SCIENCE WORKSHOP SERIES

EARTH SCIENCE
The Universe

Annotated Teacher's Edition

Seymour Rosen

GLOBE BOOK COMPANY
A Division of Simon & Schuster
Englewood Cliffs, New Jersey

ISBN: 0–8359–0389–3

Printed in the United States of America

2 3 4 5 6 7 8 9 10   95   94   93   92   91

CONTENTS

INTRODUCTION TO THE SERIES

Overview

The *Science Workshop Series* consists of 12 softbound workbooks that provide a basic secondary-school science program for students achieving below grade level. General competency in the areas of biology, earth science, chemistry, and physical science is stressed. The series is designed so that the books may be used sequentially within or across each of these science areas.

Each workbook consists of approximately 30 lessons. Each lesson opens with a manageable amount of text for students to read. The succeeding pages contain exercises, many of which include photographs or drawings. The illustrations provide students with answers to simple questions. Phonetic spellings and simple definitions for scientific terms are also included to aid in the assimilation of new words.

The question material is varied and plentiful. Exercises such as *Completing Sentences, Matching,* and *True or False* are used to reinforce material covered in the lesson. An open-ended *Reaching Out* question often completes the lesson with a slightly more challenging, yet answerable question.

Easy-to-do laboratory experiments are also included in some lessons. Not isolated, the experiments are part of the development of concepts. They are practical experiments, which require only easily obtainable, inexpensive materials.

Numerous illustrations and photographs play an important role in the development of concepts as well. The functional art enhances students' understanding and relates scientific concepts to students' daily lives.

The workbook format meets the needs of the reluctant student. The student is given a recognizable format, short lessons, and questions that are not overwhelming. The student can handle the stepwise sequence of question material in each lesson with confidence.

The series meets the needs of teachers as well. The workbooks can either be used for an entire class simultaneously, or since the lessons are self-contained, the books can be used on an individual basis for remedial purposes. This works well because the tone of each book is informal; a direct dialogue is established between the book and the student.

Using the Books

Although each lesson's reading selection may be read as part of a homework assignment, it will prove most effective if it is read during class time. This allows for an introduction to a new topic and a possible discussion. Teacher demonstrations that help to reinforce the ideas stressed in the reading should also be done during class time.

The developmental question material that follows the reading can serve as an ideal follow-up to do in class. The exercises such as *Completing Sentences, True or False* or *Matching* might be assigned for homework or used as a short quiz. The *Reaching Out* question might also be assigned for homework or completed in class to end a topic with a discussion.

Objectives

The aim of the Science Workshop Series is to increase the student's level of competency in two areas: *Science Skills* and *Verbal Skills*. The comprehensive skills matrix on page T-2 highlights the science skills that are used in each lesson.

SKILLS MATRIX

Lesson	Identifying	Classifying	Observing	Measuring	Inferring	Interpreting	Predicting	Modeling	Organizing	Analyzing	Understanding Direct and Indirect Relationships	Inductive Reasoning	Deductive Reasoning
1	●				●		●				●		
2	●				●		●						
3	●	●				●				●			●
4	●				●		●						
5	●		●	●									
6	●	●	●			●		●		●		●	
7	●				●		●			●			
8	●				●		●			●			
9	●				●			●					●
10		●						●		●			
11	●		●							●			
12	●		●	●		●	●			●			
13	●		●			●			●	●		●	●
14			●		●	●	●			●	●		●
15													
16	●		●		●					●	●		●
17	●	●	●		●	●		●		●	●		
18	●					●	●			●	●		
19	●		●		●		●			●			
20	●		●			●				●			
21	●	●	●	●					●	●			
22	●	●										●	
23	●	●											●
24	●	●										●	
25	●		●			●	●						
26	●												
27	●				●		●						
28	●				●		●				●		

VERBAL SKILLS

An important objective of the *Science Workshop Series* is to give all students—even those with reading difficulties—a certain degree of science literacy. Reading science materials is often more difficult for poor readers because of its special vocabulary. Taking this into account, each new word is introduced, defined, used in context, and repeated in order to increase its familiarity. The development of the vocabulary word **rotation** is traced below to illustrate the usage of science words in the text.

1. The word **rotation** is first defined and spelled phonetically in Lesson 10 on page 51.
2. Students identify whether an action is an example of **rotation** on page 54.
3. Exercises on pages 57-61 require students to use the word **rotation** in context.
4. The word is reintroduced and used throughout Lesson 16, which covers the rotation of the moon.

This stepwise development allows students to gradually increase their working science vocabulary.

Other techniques used to familiarize students with a specialized vocabulary are less formal and allow the student to have fun while reinforcing what has been learned. Several varieties of word games are used. For example:

- A *Crossword Puzzle* appears on page 102.
- A *Word Search* appears on page 176.
- A *Word Scramble* appears on page 164.

LANGUAGE DIVERSE POPULATIONS

Students with limited English proficiency may encounter difficulties with the core material as well as the language. Teachers of these students need to use ample repetition, simple explanations of key concepts, and many concrete examples from the students' world. Relying on information students already possess helps students gain confidence and establishes a positive learning environment.

To help LDP students with language development, it is important to maintain an open dialogue between the students and the teacher. Encourage student participation. Have students submit written and oral reports. After students read a section of the text, have them explain it in their own words. These strategies will help the teacher be aware of problem areas.

CONCEPT DEVELOPMENT

In each book the lessons are arranged in such a way as to provide a logical sequence that students can easily follow. Let us trace the development of one concept from the workbook: *Planets revolve around the sun.*

Lesson 1 familiarizes students with the concept of revolving. The fact that the earth revolves around the sun and that the moon revolves around the earth is introduced. In lesson 10, the revolution of the earth around the sun is contrasted with its rotation on its axis. Lesson 14 explains the effect of the earth's revolving on the seasons.

SAFETY IN THE SCIENCE LABORATORY

Many of the lessons in the books of the *Science Workshop Series* include easy-to-do laboratory experiments. In order to have a safe laboratory environment, there are certain rules and procedures that must be followed. It is the responsibility of every science teacher to explain safety rules and procedures to students and to make sure that students adhere to these safety rules.

To help students develop an awareness of safety in the science laboratory, a list of Safety Symbols and warnings is included at the end of this workshop.

USING THE TEACHER'S EDITION

The Teacher's Edition of *Earth Science – The Universe* has on-page annotations for all questions, exercises, charts, tables, and so on. It also includes front matter with teaching suggestions for each lesson in the book. Every lesson begins with questions to motivate the lesson. The motivational questions relate to the lesson opener pictures and provide a springboard for discussion of the lesson's science concepts. Following the *Motivation* are a variety of teaching strategies. Suggestions for *Class Activities*, *Demonstrations*, *Extensions*, *Reinforcements*, and *Cooperative/Collaborative Learning* opportunities are given.

The teacher's edition also includes a two-page test, which includes at least one question from each lesson in the book. The test can be photocopied and distributed to students. It begins on the next page. The test's Answer Key is found below.

ANSWER KEY FOR REVIEW TEST

Multiple Choice

1. b   2. a   3. a   4. a   5. d   6. a   7. d   8. d   9. a   10. b

Fill In The Blank

1. light year   2. ten trillion   3. shift position   4. reaction   5. rotates   6. ellipse
7. gas giants   8. Milky Way galaxy   9. brightness   10. oxygen

True Or False

1. false   2. true   3. false   4. true   5. true   6. true   7. true   8. true
9. false   10. false

Matching

1. g   2. e   3. i   4. b   5. f   6. c   7. h   8. d   9. a   10. j

REVIEW TEST

MULTIPLE CHOICE

In the space provided, write the letter of the word or words that best complete each statement.

_____ 1. Gravity is a
a) pushing force.   b) pulling force.   c) electrical force.   d) magnetic force.

_____ 2. On June 21, the northern hemisphere faces
a) towards the sun.   b) neither towards nor away from the sun.   c) away from the sun.   d) towards the moon.

_____ 3. At new moon, we
a) cannot see the moon.   b) see a little bit of the moon.   c) can see the back side of the moon.   d) can see one whole side of the moon.

_____ 4. A solar eclipse takes place during a
a) full moon.   b) new moon.   c) gibbous moon.   d) crescent moon.

_____ 5. The smallest planet in the solar system is
a) Mercury.   b) Earth.   c) Io.   d) Pluto.

_____ 6. The largest planet in the solar system is
a) Jupiter.   b) Saturn.   c) Uranus.   d) Neptune.

_____ 7. The middle of the sun is called the
a) corona.   b) photosphere.   c) chromosphere.   d) core.

_____ 8. Mercury, Venus and Earth
a) have rings.   b) are gas giants.   c) have no moons.   d) are terrestrial planets.

_____ 9. Jupiter, Saturn, Uranus, and Neptune
a) have rings.   b) have oceans.   c) have no moons.   d) are terrestrial planets

_____ 10. The first planet visited by *Voyager 1* and *Voyager 2* was:
a) Mars.   b) Jupiter.   c) Saturn.   d) Neptune.

FILL IN THE BLANK

Complete each statement using a term from the list below. Write your answers in the spaces provided.

| light year | shift position | reaction | ten trillion | rotates |
| ellipse | gas giants | Milky Way galaxy | brightness | oxygen |

1. A _____ is the distance that light travels in one year.

2. One light year is equal to about _____ kilometers.

3. Every object seems to_____ when seen from two different places.

4. The *Third Law of Motion* states that for every action, there is a _____ .

5. Earth _____ on its axis.

6. The shape of Earth's orbit around the sun is an _____ .

7. Jupiter, Saturn, Uranus and Neptune are _____ .

8. Our solar system is part of the _____ .

9. Stars can vary in their color and their _____ .

10. A space craft must provide astronauts with _____ .

TRUE OR FALSE

In the space provided, write "true" if the sentence is true. Write "false" is the sentence is false.

_____ 1. The sun revolves around the Earth.

_____ 2. The moon revolves around the Earth.

_____ 3. The Space Shuttle takes off like an airplane.

_____ 4. The Space Shuttle lands like an airplane.

_____ 5. The Earth rotates around the sun.

_____ 6. The time in Los Angeles is earlier than the time in New York.

_____ 7. The moon and Earth pull on each other because of gravity.

_____ 8. You can only see one side of the moon from Earth.

_____ 9. The moon gives off its own light.

_____ 10. During a lunar eclipse, the moon is behind the sun.

MATCHING

Match each term in Column A with its description in Column B. Write the correct letter in the space provided.

Column A		Column B	
_____ 1. Galileo		a)	is between Mars and Jupiter
_____ 2. *Viking*		b)	analyzes light
_____ 3. tides		c)	explored outer planets
_____ 4. spectrascope		d)	orbit planets
_____ 5. Newton		e)	landed on Mars
_____ 6. *Voyager*		f)	wrote the *Third Law of Motion*
_____ 7. fusion		g)	made first practical use of telescope
_____ 8. moons		h)	powers the sun
_____ 9. asteroid belt		i)	caused by the gravitational pull of the sun and moon
_____ 10. Polaris		j)	North Star

LESSON TEACHING STRATEGIES

LESSON 1

Why do we study space? (pp. 1-6)

Motivation   Refer students to the lesson opener picture on page 1 and ask the following questions:

1. What is the boy in the picture looking at?

2. What is the object on the right?

Class Activity   To motivate this lesson, have your class debate whether life exists elsewhere in the universe. Point out that space exploration may some day answer this question.

Discussion   Tell students that the government spends billions of dollars on the space program. Have students suggest reasons for this interest. List student responses on the chalkboard. Some possibilities include: learn more about the universe, explore the moon and the planets, conduct experiments to find out how to maintain life in space, search for life on the other planets, improve methods of forecasting weather, improve national defense, test various scientific laws, produce better methods of communication, develop a better understanding of how other bodies in space affect our planet.

LESSON 2

What is a telescope? (pp. 7-11)

Motivation   Refer students to the lesson opener picture on page 7 and ask the following questions:

1. What is the girl in the picture doing?

2. What is the large object in the background?

Discussion   Refer students to the diagram of a simple refracting telescope on page 10. Explain how a refracting telescope works. Have students identify the objective and eyepiece lenses. Describe how each lens works.

Discussion   Using the illustration on page 10 as a guide, draw a reflecting telescope on the chalkboard. Point out the locations of the mirrors and lenses in the telescope. Then compare and contrast a reflecting telescope and a refracting telescope.

Class Activity   Have students construct a simple reflecting telescope. Direct them to mount a screen at the center of ruler and to aim the ruler at some distant object. Using a concave mirror, demonstrate how to focus the image of the distant object on the screen. Allow students to observe and describe the image formed on the screen. Have the screen extended to one side of the stick and the mirror placed at a slight angle in order to produce a better image. Ask students to observe and describe the image formed by the mirror. Then demonstrate how to view the image formed by the mirror through the convex lens. Have students observe and describe the image formed.

Extension   Have interested students find out more about Hans Lippershey or Galileo. Tell students to write a brief biography about their lives.

Reinforcement   Have a student stand outside the classroom and ring a bell. Ask students what object is making the noise. (a bell) Point out that students cannot see the bell, but that they know it is a bell because of its sound. Relate this activity to the way radio telescopes are used to study stars.

LESSON 3

What is a spectroscope? (pp. 13-18)

Motivation   Refer students to the lesson opener picture on page 13 and ask the following questions:

1. What is happening to the light passing through the prism?

2. What is special about fingerprints?

Demonstration   Direct a light through a prism and project a spectrum onto a screen. Have the students identify the colors of the spectrum.

Discussion   Explain how scientists use a spectroscope to study stars. Point out that each element has its own spectrum. Have students observe the different spectra of the elements on page 17. Compare the method of identifying elements through their spectra with the method of identifying individuals through their fingerprints.

LESSON 4

How do astronomers measure distances? (pp. 19-22)

Motivation Refer students to the lesson opener picture on page 19 and ask the following questions:

1. How far is it from the earth to the sun?

2. How far is it from the sun to the nearest star?

Discussion Point out that distances on Earth can be measured in centimeters, meters, or kilometers, but because distances in space are so great, much larger units than those used for ordinary purposes are needed to measure these distances. Introduce the light year and astronomical units as units of measurements used by astronomers.

Class Activity Using the given speed of light, 300,000 km / sec, lead students through the mathematical calculations necessary to determine the distance light travels in one year.

Discussion Define astronomical unit as the distance between the earth and the sun, or 150 million kilometers. Refer students to Figure A on page 21 to observe the distance of planets from the sun in astronomical units. Point out that Mercury and Venus are less than 1 AU from the sun, and therefore are closer to the sun than Earth.

LESSON 5

What is parallax? (pp. 23-26)

Motivation Refer students to the lesson opener picture on page 23 and ask the following questions:

1. What is the boy in the picture doing?

2. What is the difference between the two pictures of the building and the finger?

Reinforcement The concept of parallax often is hard for students to understand. Review this concept with students until they can understand it.

LESSON 6

How does a rocket move? (pp. 27-32)

Motivation Refer students to the lesson opener picture on page 27 and ask the following questions:

1. Which direction is the rocket moving?

2. Which direction are the flames coming out of the rocket moving?

Reinforcement Write Newton's *Third Law of Motion* on the chalkboard: "For every action, there is an equal reaction in the opposite direction." Ask students for examples which illustrate this law. (Possible responses include a recoiling rifle, jumping off a small boat, and a rotating lawn sprinkler.)

Discussion Refer students to the diagram of a rocket on page 30. Point out the different parts of a rocket and describe a rocket's thrust.

LESSON 7

What are satellites and space probes? (pp. 33-38)

Motivation Refer students to the lesson opener picture on page 33 and ask the following questions:

1. What planet is shown in the picture?

2. What is the spacecraft in the picture doing?

Discussion You may wish to tell students that the exploration of space began in 1957, as part of the International Geophysical Year (IGY). The International Geophysical Year was planned as a year of astronomical observations by scientists of many countries.

Reinforcement Remind students that Sputnik was launched as part of the International Geophysical Year.

Discussion Describe how artificial satellites and space probes are used to explore space. Be sure students understand the advantages of space probes.

Class Activity If possible, arrange for your class to visit a space museum where rockets, satellites, or space probes are on display.

Extension You may wish to tell students that the thirty-fifth anniversary of the International Geophysical Year will be celebrated in 1992. That year will be called the International Space Year, or ISY. Space missions during the ISY will not study other planets or distant galaxies. The main goal of the ISY is to study Earth.

LESSON 8

What is a space shuttle? (pp. 39-44)

Motivation Refer students to the lesson opener picture on page 39 and ask the following questions:

1. What does the Space Shuttle look like when it takes off?

2. How does the Space Shuttle land?

Cooperative/Collaborative Learning Have a volunteer describe some of the uses of the Space Shuttle to the rest of the class.

LESSON 9

How do humans survive in space (pp. 45-50)

Motivation Refer students to the lesson opener picture on page 45 and ask the following questions:

1. Why are the astronauts shown here wearing space suits?

2. What is the astronaut on the left experiencing that the other astronaut is not experiencing?

Class Discussion Use this lesson to emphasize how space exploration benefits people. Discuss the many spinoffs (such as freeze dried food, lightweight clothing, nonstick pans, and smaller, lighter electronic equipment) that have resulted from space exploration.

Reinforcement Most students find the concept of "weightlessness" hard to understand. Make sure students understand this concept.

Cooperative/Collaborative Learning Have student volunteers describe to the class how they would perform a daily task, such as eating or sleeping, in an environment with little or no gravity.

LESSON 10

What are the earth's motions? (pp. 51-54)

Motivation Refer students to the lesson opener picture on page 51 and ask the following questions:

1. What motion of the earth is shown in the bottom left picture?

2. What motion of the earth is shown in the bottom right picture?

Demonstration Demonstrate rotation by spinning a globe on its axis.

Extension You may want to explain to students that there is proof of the earth's rotation. For example, you may want to explain the use of time exposure photographs of stars. The use of a pendulum is another way scientists can prove that the earth is moving. Ask students if any of them have ever seen the pendulum hanging in the Smithsonian Institute in Washington, D.C.

LESSON 11

What causes day and night? (pp. 55-62)

Motivation Refer students to the lesson opener picture on page 55 and ask the following questions:

1. What are the differences in these two pictures?

2. Why is there light during daytime?

Demonstration Using a globe and a lamp in a darkened room, demonstrate how rotation produces day and night.

Demonstration Using a globe, demonstrate the direction of the earth's rotation, and the apparent motion of the sun across the sky.

Discussion To introduce the lesson, write the following dates on the chalkboard: March 21, June 21, September 21, December 21. Ask students what these dates signify. (Most students will recognize these dates as the first day of Spring, Summer, Winter, and Fall, respectively.) Point out that in the Northern hemisphere June 21 is called the summer solstice, and December 21 is called the winter solstice., Describe the positions of the earth on the solstices. Then identify March 21 and September 21 as the equinoxes and describe the position of the earth on these days.

Reinforcement To help students remember that during an equinox, all places on the earth have 12 hours of darkness and 12 hours of night stress that all places have the same or equal hours of darkness and daylight.

LESSON 12

What are time zones? (pp. 63-70)

Motivation   Refer students to the lesson opener picture on page 63 and ask the following questions:

1. The two people shown here are talking to each other on the phone. Where are they?

2. What time is it in each place?

Discussion   Discuss the establishment of time zones. Discuss why time zones are important and the confusion that would result without the establishment of time zones.

Reinforcement   Using a globe or map, review what is meant by meridian or longitude. Guide the class to see that the earth moves through 360° during one complete rotation. Point out that a day is divided into 24 hours. Develop the idea that there is one hour difference for each 15° of longitude (360°/24 = 15°).

Class Activity   Using the map on page 67, locate and identify the time zones in the continental United States. Then have students take turns reading out the names of any two places in the United States in different time zones. Tell students to write a sample time for the first place they name on the chalkboard. Have the rest of the class determine the time in the other place.

LESSON 13

How does the earth orbit the sun? (pp. 71-76)

Motivation   Refer students to the lesson opener picture on page 71 and ask the following questions:

1. In the picture, is the earth always the same distance from the sun?

2. Does the earth move in a circle around the sun?

Reteaching Option   Draw an ellipse on the chalkboard and have students describe its shape. Label the major axis and foci of the ellipse. Explain that the earth travels in an elliptical orbit around the sun. Point out that the sun is located at one focus of the ellipse. Label the sun on your diagram. Have a student draw in a circle to represent the earth.

Discussion   Describe the difference between a circle and an ellipse. Explain that the earth's orbit around the sun is elliptical. Guide students to see that because the earth's orbit is an ellipse, the distance between the earth and sun is not always the same. Discuss perihelion and aphelion.

Reinforcement   Have students recall that the astronomical unit (AU) is equal to 150,000,000 kilometers, or the average distance from the earth to the sun. Tell students that the earth is sometimes more than 150,000,000 km from the sun, and is sometimes less than 150,000,000 km.

Demonstration   Throw a small object in the air. Ask students why the object falls to the ground. (Gravity pulls the object toward the earth.) Point out that on the earth gravity pulls all objects toward the earth.

LESSON 14

What causes the change of season? (pp. 77-82)

Motivation   Refer students to the lesson opener picture on page 77 and ask the following questions:

1. What season is it in the picture on the left?

2. What season is it in the picture on the right?

Reinforcement   Be sure students understand that changes in the distance between the earth and sun do not cause the seasons. Ask students what month the earth is at perihelion (January). Point out that the Northern Hemisphere has winter in January.

Discussion   Using the diagram on page 80, discuss the earth's tilt and seasons. Explain the relationship between direct rays, slanted rays, and the seasons. Point out that the angle of the sun's rays and the length of day determine the seasons.

Discussion   Ask students if there are more daylight hours in the winter or in the summer. (summer) Have students try to explain why. Discuss all student responses. Explain that the earth's axis is tilted. Guide students to see that the number of daylight hours changes because the earth's axis is tilted.

LESSON 15

What is known about the earth's moon? (pp. 83-88)

Motivation Refer students to the lesson opener picture on page 83 and ask the following questions:

1. What is shown in this picture?

2. Have people ever visited the moon?

Discussion Display photographs of the moon and ask students to identify it. Then describe the characteristics of the moon. Have students describe the various features they see, such as mountains, craters, and plains.

Reinforcement Be sure students understand the proper use of the term "moon." Point out that other planets have natural satellites, or moons but that the earth is the only planet with a satellite named Moon.

Extension Have interested students find out more about *Project Apollo*. Tell students to write their findings in a report.

LESSON 16

Why can we see only one side of the moon? (pp. 89-96)

Motivation Refer students to the lesson opener picture on page 89 and ask the following questions:

1. What are the two objects in this picture?

2. What is happening in this picture?

Class Activity Have students collect newspapers listing the times the moon rises for the next week. After a week, have students compare the times. Tell them to note that the moon rises 50 minutes later each day.

Demonstration Using a large slate globe, guide students to see why people only see one side of the moon. Divide the globe into four equal sections by drawing lines form pole to pole. Shine a light on the globe, and demonstrate that each part is illuminated at one time or another. Walk around the room and slowly rotate the globe, so that the same side faces the class throughout your "revolution."

LESSON 17

What are the phases of the moon? (pp. 97-102)

Motivation Refer students to the lesson opener picture on page 97 and ask the following questions:

1. Is the same object shown in all three of these photographs?

2. Which photo shows a full moon?

Discussion Display a calendar and have the students note the dates of new, full, first-, and last-quarter moons. Point out that these are the phases of the moon. Explain why the moon appears to change shape.

Demonstration Demonstrate the phases of the moon by shining a projector on a globe. Tell students the projector represents the sun. Then attach a styrofoam ball to a pencil to represent the moon. Using the diagram on page 99 as a guide, hold the ball at different positions around the globe. Tell students to note that only certain parts of the ball are lighted at the different positions.

Extension Assign a moon observation for the next four weeks. Have students keep a record of the phases, and the time and date each occurs. Encourage them to make drawings of how the moon appears each night.

LESSON 18

What is a solar eclipse? (pp. 103-109)

Motivation Refer students to the lesson opener picture on page 103 and ask the following questions:

1. What is happening to the sun in this picture?

2. What is blocking the light of the sun in this picture?

Demonstration Place an object on a piece of white paper, and hold it in front of a lamp. Have students observe the shadow that is formed. Point out the umbra and penumbra of the shadow.

Discussion Refer students to the diagrams showing a solar eclipse on page 105. Explain how solar eclipses occur and why a solar eclipse varies at different places on earth.

Extension Caution students to never look directly at the sun, even during a solar eclipse.

LESSON 19

What is a lunar eclipse? (pp. 111-116)

Motivation   Refer students to the lesson opener picture on page 111 and ask the following questions:

1. What is happening to the moon in this picture?

2. What is blocking the sun's light from hitting the moon in this picture?

Discussion   Using the diagram on page 113, describe a lunar eclipse.

Class Activity   Divide the class into small groups. Distribute a softball, a small styrofoam (or ping-pong) ball, and a light source to each group. Direct students to shine the light on the softball (earth) and then place the ping-pong ball (moon) in the umbra of the softball. **Caution students not to look directly into the light.** Darken the room as much as possible and check to see that the light from one group does not interfere with that of other groups.

Cooperative/Collaborative Learning   Have one student compare a lunar eclipse and a solar eclipse.

LESSON 20

What causes tides? (pp. 117-124)

Motivation   Refer students to the lesson opener picture on page 117 and ask the following questions:

1. What is different in the two pictures?

2. Which picture shows high tide?

Discussion   Display a tide table from a newspaper, almanac, or fishing magazine. Point out that the tides are daily changes in the level of the earth's oceans and seas, and relate the changes of tides to students' experiences at the beach. Have students note that the time between high tide and low tide is approximately six hours, and that high tide and low tide occur twice each day.

Reinforcement   Remind students that the gravitational attraction between two objects is directly related to the distance between them. This will help students understand why the side of the earth facing the moon has a high tide. Then point out that low tides are produced by the movement of water to high tide locations.

Extension   An indirect high tide is produced on the opposite side of the earth as a result of the moon's pull on the solid earth The earth responds to the moon's gravity by moving slightly toward the moon. As the solid earth moves, the water on the side of the earth farthest from the moon is "left behind," resulting in a high tide on that side of the moon.

LESSON 21

What is the solar system? (pp. 125-130)

Motivation   Refer students to the lesson opener picture on page 125 and ask the following questions:

1. What planets do you recognize in this picture?

2. What are the planets circling in this picture?

Reinforcement   Refer students to the diagram of the solar system on page 127. Randomly read out the names of the planets. Have students locate each planet and classify it as an inner or outer planet.

LESSON 22

What are the features of the sun? (pp. 131-136)

Motivation   Refer students to the lesson opener picture on page 131 and ask the following questions:

1. What is shown in this picture?

2. Why should you never look directly at the sun?

Class Activity   Have students work in pairs to construct charts comparing the parts of the sun.

Reinforcement   Using the diagram on page 134 as a guide, draw a cross section of the sun on the chalkboard. Have students come up to the chalkboard and label the core, photosphere, chromosphere, and corona.

Discussion   Refer students to the photographs of sunspots, and a solar flare on page 135, and discuss each of these features of the sun.

Extension   Graphs of sunspot cycles have been made since before 1700. Obtain tables containing sunspot numbers to illustrate sunspot cycles. Have students plot and graph the number of sunspots for each year. Tell them to note how the number of sunspots increases over a period of 10-11 years.

LESSON 23

What are the inner planets? (pp. 137-144)

Motivation   Refer students to the lesson opener picture on page 137 and ask the following questions:

1.   Which planet has white polar ice caps?

2.   Which planet has a thick cloudy atmosphere?

Discussion   Identify Mercury, Venus, Earth, and Mars as the four inner planets. Describe the characteristics of these planets.

Class Activity   Divide the class into small groups. Have each group construct a chart describing and comparing the characteristics of the inner planets. Display the charts in the classroom.

LESSON 24

What are the outer planets? (pp. 145-152)

Motivation   Refer students to the lesson opener picture on page 145 and ask the following questions:

1.   Which planet has a great red spot?

2.   Which planet has many rings?

Discussion   Describe the characteristics of Jupiter and Saturn. Have students observe the photographs of Jupiter and Saturn on pages 147 and 148. Tell them to note the Great Red Spot of Jupiter and the rings around Saturn.

Extension   The Great Red Spot on Jupiter is similar to hot spots on the earth The earth's hot spots produce eruptions of magma. The hot spot of Jupiter produces eruptions of gases.

Cooperative/Collaborative Learning   Have a volunteer compare Jupiter and Saturn for the rest of the class.

Discussion   Describe the characteristics of Uranus, Neptune, and Pluto. Have students observe the photographs of these planets on pages 149, 150, and 151.

Extension   Pluto has been inside the orbit of Neptune since January 22, 1979.

Extension   Students have now learned about all nine planets. Tell students to write an essay titled "A Trip through the Solar System." Have them imagine that they are leaving the earth in a spaceshiip that will take them to the Moon and all the other planets. Tell students to write a description of what they will see on their journey.

LESSON 25

What are stars? (pp. 153-158)

Motivation   Refer students to the lesson opener picture on page 153 and ask the following questions:

1.   What does this picture show?

2.   What is the star in our solar system called?

Class Activity   Motivate this lesson by asking students what they would like to know about stars. Remind students that the sun is a star. Distribute one index card to each student. Tell students to write down one question they have about stars. Collect all the cards in a shoebox. After completing this unit, have students answer as many of the questions as they can.

Discussion   Describe the composition and formation of stars.

Demonstration   Display a classroom chart of the Hertzsprung-Russel diagram. Using the H-R diagram, explain to students how stars are classified. Explain how color, size, and absolute magnitude are used to place a star on the diagram and to identify it as a red giant, supergiant, white dwarf, or main sequence star. Then have students classify the stars using the H-R diagram.

LESSON 26

How do stars get their energy? (pp. 159-164)

Motivation   Refer students to the lesson opener picture on page 159 and ask the following questions:

1.   What is shown in the top left picture?

2.   What happens to the hydrogen atoms in the pictures?

Reinforcement   Students may recall that nuclear energy is being used in some places to produce electricity Be sure students understand that reactions taking place in nuclear power plants involve breaking apart atoms. Point out that fusion is a nuclear reaction that involves joining atoms.

Extension To explain the differences between an ordinary chemical reation, such as oxidation, and a nuclear reaction, such as the fission of uranium atoms or the fusion of hydrogen atoms, you may wish to go into the structure of the atom. In chemical reations, only the electrons of atoms are involved. They change their positions and may give up some energy. This is the energy given off by reactions such as burning. Nuclear reactions involve changes in the nuclei of atoms and the energies involved are many times greater.

Discussion Write Einstein's formula $E = mc^2$ on the chalkboard. Explain in terms of the equation how mass can be changed to energy. Point out that "c" is the speed of light, and that this large number is squared in the formula. That explains why very small changes in mass can result in enormous amounts of energy.

LESSON 27

What are constellations? (pp. 165-169)

Motivation Refer students to the lesson opener picture on page 165 and ask the following questions:

1. What shape is drawn over the stars in this picture?

2. Can you really see these shapes if you look at these stars in the sky?

Discussion To introduce this lesson, write the following terms on the chalkboard: Aquarius, Leo, Pisces, Ursa Major, Ursa Minor, Orion, Capricorn, Libra. Ask students if they recognize any of these names. (Students may recognize some of the names as zodiac signs.) Point out that the terms are the names of constellations. Discuss what a constellation is. Then point out that zodiac signs are named for constellations that occupy a specific region of the sky.

Reinforcement Remind students of the importance of establishing standards in the naming of constellations. It makes communication among scientists all over the world easier.

Extension Use a current issue of *Sky and Telescope* to determine what constellations are visible. Have interested students look for the constellations and sketch any star groups they observe.

LESSON 28

What are galaxies? (pp. 171-176)

Motivation Refer students to the lesson opener picture on page 171 and ask the following questions:

1. What shape do the stars seem to be in?

2. How many stars do you think there are in this picture?

Class Activity Write the following head on the chalkboard: GALAXIES. From this head, draw arrows to each of the following heads: SPIRAL GALAXY, ELLIPTICAL GALAXY, IRREGULAR GALAXY. Describe the shape of each type of galaxy. Tell students to copy the information in their notebooks under the proper head.

Reinforcement Obtain as many photographs and drawings of the three kinds of galaxies as possible. Hold up each picture in front of the class. Have students classify each galaxy according to its shape.

Extension Examples of spiral galaxies are the Milky Way, Andromeda, and the Whirlpool galaxy. Examples of elliptical galaxies are NGD 205, NGC 221 found in the constellation Andromeda and NGC 3193 found in the constellation Leo. NGC stands for the New General Catalogue, which lists galaxies with a number. Examples of irregular galaxies include the Large Magellanic Cloud, the Small Magellanic Cloud, and NGC 5195. Have interested students find out more about one of these galaxies. Tell students to write their findings in a report.

Discussion Review the different types of galaxies. Point out that the Milky Way galaxy is a spiral galaxy. Using a photograph of a spiral galaxy (M 51 is a good example), review the characteristics of this type of galaxy. Be sure students understand the difference between the Milky Way galaxy and the Milky Way.

SCIENCE WORKSHOP SERIES
EARTH SCIENCE
The Universe

Seymour Rosen

GLOBE BOOK COMPANY
A Division of Simon & Schuster
Englewood Cliffs, New Jersey

THE AUTHOR

Seymour Rosen received his B.A. and M.S. degrees from Brooklyn College. He taught science in the New York City School System for twenty-seven years. Mr. Rosen was also a contributing participant in a teacher-training program for the development of science curriculum for the New York City Board of Education.

Cover Photograph: Digital Art/Westlight
Photo Researcher: Rhoda Sidney

Photo Credits:

p. 3, Fig. A: New York Public Library
p. 5, Fig. F: NASA
p. 5, Fig. G: NASA
p. 9, Fig. A: The Bettmann Archive
p. 9, Fig. B: Library of Congress
p. 11, Fig. G: National Radio Astronomy
   Observatory
p. 12: NASA
p. 21, Fig. A: Lick Observatory
p. 31, Fig. D: NASA
p. 35, Fig. A: NOAA/NEDIS/NCDC
p. 35, Fig. B: NASA
p. 35, Fig. C: NASA
p. 35, Fig. D: NASA
p. 35, Fig. E: JPL/NASA
p. 35, Fig. F: NASA
p. 42, Fig. B: NASA
p. 42, Fig. C: NASA
p. 42, Fig. D: NASA
p. 42, Fig. E: NASA
p. 43, Fig. F: NASA
p. 43, Fig. G: NASA
p. 47, Fig. A: NASA
p. 48, Fig. B: NASA
p, 48, Fig. C: NASA
p. 49, Fig. D: NASA
p. 49, Fig. E: NASA
p. 51: NASA
p. 83: Lick Observatory
p. 85, Fig. A: NASA
p. 86, Fig. B: NASA
p. 86, Fig. C: NASA
p. 86, Fig. D: NASA
p. 88, Fig. F: NASA
p. 97: Lick Observatory (all 3 photos)
p. 100, Fig. B: Lick Observatory
p. 100, Fig. C: Lick Observatory

p. 100, Fig. D: Lick Observatory
p. 100, Fig. E: Lick Observatory
p. 100, Fig. G: Lick Observatory
p. 100, Fig. H: Lick Observatory
p. 100, Fig. I: Lick Observatory
p. 103: Lick Observatory
p. 105, Fig. B: Pictorial Parade
p. 106, Fig. C: Lick Observatory
p. 106, Fig. D: UPI/Bettmann Newsphotos
p. 110: American Museum of Natural History
p. 111: Jay Pasachoff
p. 131: Joe Munroe/Photo Researchers
p. 134, Fig. D: NASA
p. 135, Fig. E: NASA
p. 137: NASA (both photos)
p. 139, Fig. A: NASA
p. 140, Fig. B: NASA
p. 141, Fig. C: NASA
p. 142, Fig. D: NASA
p. 142, Fig. E: NASA
p. 145: NASA (all 3 photos)
p. 147, Fig. A: NASA
p. 148, Fig. B: NASA
p. 149, Fig. C: NASA
p. 150, Fig. D: NASA
p. 151, Fig. E: NASA
p. 153: Lick Observatory
p. 162, Fig. D: NASA
p. 162, Fig. E: United Nations/U.S.I.A.
p. 168, Fig. E: Lick Observatory
p. 170: NASA
p. 171: Lick Observatory
p. 173, Fig. A: Lick Observatory
p. 173, Fig. B: Kitt Peak National Observatory
p. 173, Fig. C: Kitt Peak National Observatory
p. 174, Fig. D: Kitt Peak National Observatory

ISBN: 0-8359-0388-5

Printed in the United States of America
2 3 4 5 6 7 8 9 10   95 94 93 92 91

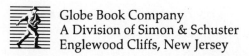
Globe Book Company
A Division of Simon & Schuster
Englewood Cliffs, New Jersey

CONTENTS

Introduction to The Universe

For thousands and thousands of years, humans have watched the sun, moon, stars and planets cross the sky each day and night. They would wonder what these heavenly bodies were and why they behaved the way that they did. Some moved in straight lines while others curved. Some move faster than others.

Today we know much more than the people who watched the sky thousands of years ago. We know that the moon revolves around the earth and that all the planets, including Earth, revolve around the sun.

In this book you will learn about the structure and motions of the planets and much more. You will learn more about the universe than could have been dreamed of a thousand years ago, or even one hundred years ago. Still, there are many things in the universe that we do not yet understand. Today, people still watch the sky and wonder.

Why do we study space? 1

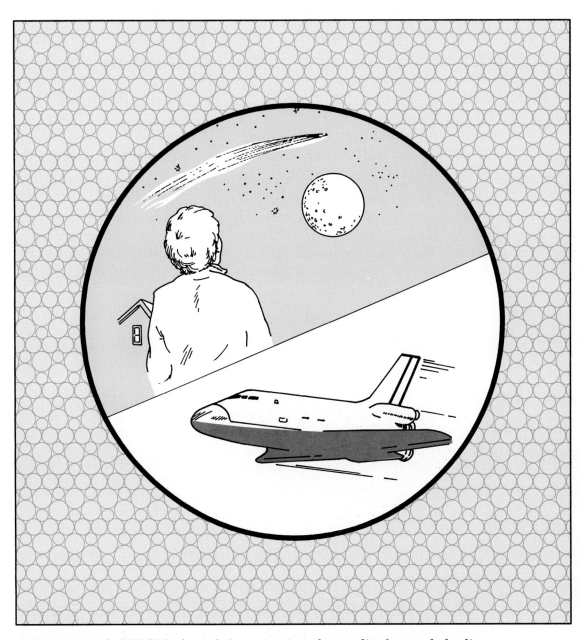

astronomer [uh-STRON-uh-muhr]:   scientist who studies heavenly bodies
astronomy [uh-STRON-uh-mee]:   study of heavenly bodies
satellite [SAT-uh-lite]:   natural or artificial object orbiting a body in space
universe [YOO-nuh-vurs]:   everything that exists

LESSON 1 | Why do we study space?

Have you ever looked deep into a evening sky? Did you wonder how far away the stars are and what lies beyond the stars. People have always wondered about the heavens. Why?

The answer lies in the natural curiosity of the human mind. We see the sky above us and ask questions. We try to figure out the answers to these questions. However, more often than not, the answers lead to more questions. The study of heavenly bodies is called **astronomy** [uh-STRON-uh-mee]. Scientists who study astronomy are called **astronomers** [uh-STRON-uh-muhrs].

When we study astronomy, we learn a little bit more about the universe. The sun, moon and planets are part of the universe. So are the stars. Everything that exists is part of the universe. So the **universe** [YOO-nuh-vurs] is everything that exists.

Earth is part of the universe. So when we learn more about the universe, we learn more about the earth's place in the universe. For example, the more we learn about the other planets in the solar system, the more we know about planets in general. As we learn more about planets in general, the better we understand the planet earth.

Figure A *Nicholas Copernicus*

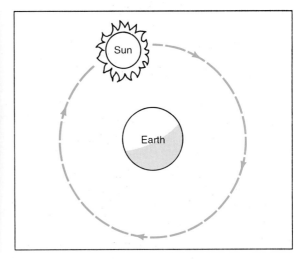

Figure B *People once thought that the sun revolved around the earth.*

For many centuries, people thought that the earth was the center of the universe. They thought that the sun and the stars revolved around the earth. The problem with this explanation was that the planets did not seem to revolve around the earth in any simple way. People made very complex models to try to explain how the planets moved around the earth.

Nicholas Copernicus (koh-PUR-nih-kus) was a Polish astronomer who lived in the 1500s. He studied the sky and made very careful observations even though he had no instruments to help him. Copernicus's studies convinced him that the earth and other planets revolved around the sun. For many years, most people did not believe his ideas. Today we know that they are true.

Copernicus's ideas changed the way humans viewed the universe. We now know that the earth is <u>not</u> the center of the universe but just one small planet among countless stars.

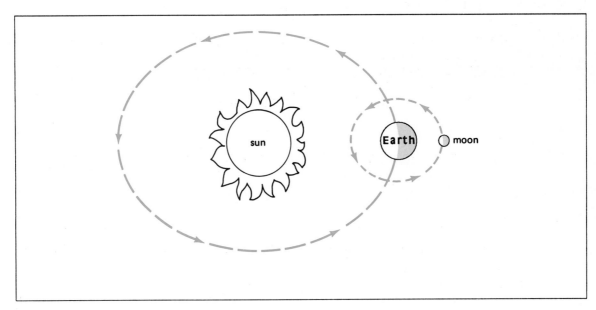

Figure C *We now know that the earth revolves around the sun.*

TRUE OR FALSE

In the space provided, write "true" if the sentence is true. Write "false" if the sentence is false.

True	**1.**	Earth is part of the universe.
False	**2.**	The sun revolves around the earth.
True	**3.**	The moon revolves around the earth.
True	**4.**	The earth revolves around the sun.
False	**5.**	Copernicus was an astronaut.
True	**6.**	The study of heavenly bodies is called astronomy.
False	**7.**	The earth used to be the center of the universe.
True	**8.**	People once that that the earth was the center of the universe.
True	**9.**	Astronomers study astronomy.
False	**10.**	Today, we know everything there is to know about space.

MATCHING

Match each term in Column A with its description in Column B. Write the correct letter in the space provided.

	Column A		**Column B**
d	**1.** astronomy	**a)**	revolves around the earth
e	**2.** earth	**b)**	planets revolve around it
b	**3.** sun	**c)**	everything that exists
a	**4.** moon	**d)**	the study of objects in space
c	**5.** universe	**e)**	revolves around the sun

Scientists do more than study space. They also send things (and people) into space. In 1957, the Soviet Union launched the first artificial satellite, called *Sputnik*, into orbit. Since that time the United States, Soviet Union, and several other countries have launched things into orbit around the Earth. There are a number of reasons to put people and satellites into orbit.

Figure D *Space probes*

Figure E *Communication satellites*

Figure F *Experiments in zero gravity*

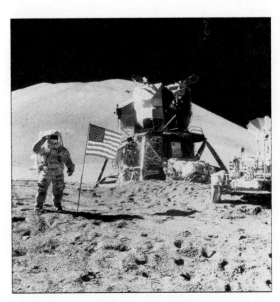

Figure G *Sending people into space*

FILL IN THE BLANK

Complete each statement using a term or terms from the list below. Write your answers in the spaces provided. Some words may be used more than once.

earth	astronomers	1957
sun	the 1500s	satellite
Soviet Union	Polish	

1. The _____earth_____ revolves around the _____sun_____ .

2. The moon revolves around the _____earth_____ .

3. _____Astronomers_____ study objects in space.

4. Copernicus lived in _____the 1500s_____ .

5. Sputnik was launched in _____1957_____ .

6. Sputnik was a _____satellite_____ .

7. Copernicus was a _____Polish_____ astronomer.

8. Sputnik was launched by the _____Soviet Union_____ .

9. Planets revolve around the _____sun_____ .

10. Satellites orbit the _____earth_____ .

REACHING OUT

Some people believe that society should build places for people to live in space. Why might people want society to do this. _____Answers will vary. Possible answers include that there is not enough room on Earth for all the people or that there is work for people to do in space._____

What is a telescope? | 2

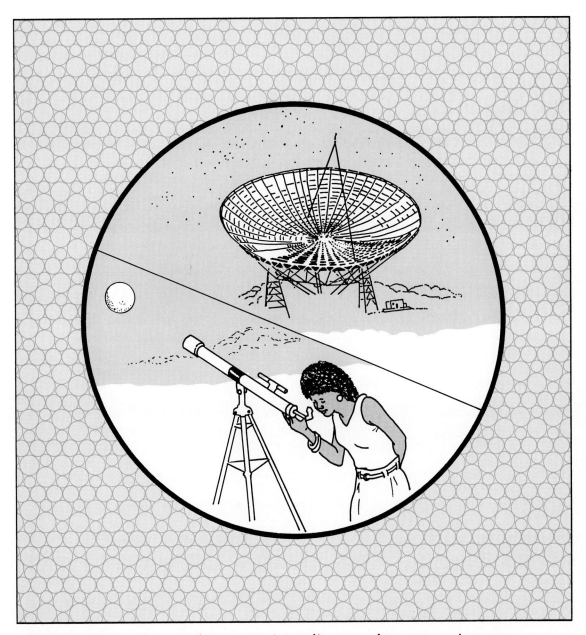

radio telescope: telescope that can receive radio waves from sources in space
reflecting [rih-FLEKT-ing] **telescope:** telescope that uses a concave mirror to collect light and produce an enlarged image
refracting [rih-FRAKT-ing] **telescope:** telescope that uses convex lenses to collect light and produce an enlarged image
telescope: an instrument that gathers and magnifies light; used to study the heavens

LESSON 2 | What is a telescope?

American astronauts have walked on the moon. But long before they did, telescopes gave us a good idea of what the moon's surface looks like.

You can see the planet Saturn with your eyes alone. But you cannot see its rings. A telescope shows the rings clearly.

Jupiter is visible to the naked eye, too. But you cannot see its moons. Using even a low-power telescope, you can see four of its moons. But with a high-power telescope you can find that there are at least eight more.

There is no questions about it . . . The most useful tool in astronomy is the **telescope**.

There are two main types of telescopes: optical telescopes and the radio telescopes.

OPTICAL TELESCOPES   An optical telescope is an instrument that gathers and magnifies light from faraway places. It makes distant objects seem much larger and closer than they really are.

There are two kinds of optical telescopes:

- A **refracting** [rih-FRAKT-ing] **telescope** uses **lenses** to gather light. A lens is a curved piece of glass. When a beam of light passes through a lens, the light is focused to a single point.

- A **reflecting** [rih-FLEKT-ing] **telescope** uses a curved mirror.

RADIO TELESCOPES   A radio telescope does not gather visible light. Instead, a radio telescope gathers invisible radio energy from objects deep in space. The signals give us clues about the location and makeup of the objects.

Figure A *Hans Lippershey*

Figure B *Galileo*

The optical telescope was invented in 1608 by a Dutch lens maker named Hans Lippershey. Strange as it seems, he was refused a patent.

An Italian astronomer named Galileo made the first practical use of Lippershey's invention. In 1609, Galileo made his first telescope. It was crude and low powered. It enabled him to make important discoveries. Galileo was the first person to see mountains and craters on the moon, the rings of Saturn, and four of Jupiter's moons.

Figure C *Galileo used his telescope to see things that were not visible to the naked eye.*

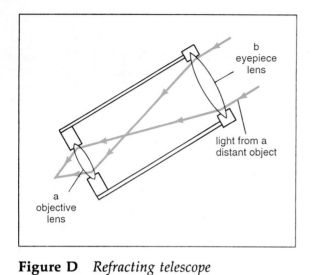

Figure D *Refracting telescope*

Refracting telescopes have two lenses. The objective lens is closer to the object being observed. The eyepiece lens is closer to the eye of the person looking through the telescope.

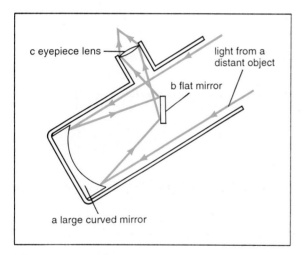

Figure E *Reflecting telescope*

Reflecting telescopes use a curved mirror instead of an objective lens. A curved mirror focuses the light rays the same way that a lens does. A flat mirror is used to change the direction the light is traveling.

Since scientists can make very large mirrors, very large reflecting telescopes can be made. Some telescopes have mirrors that are 4 meters (12 feet) wide.

Figure F *Camera attached to a telescope*

Sometimes, a camera is attached to a telescope so that pictures of objects in space can be taken. The camera "looks" through the telescope just as a person would and a picture is taken. The pictures are then studied.

Radio telescopes work like reflecting telescopes. Instead of having a mirror, radio telescopes have large radio dishes. Instead of reflecting visible light, radio dishes reflect radio waves. The radio waves are recorded by a detector into a computer just as light is recorded by a camera onto film.

Figure G *Radio telescope*

MATCHING

Match each term in Column A with its description in Column B. Write the correct letter in the space provided.

	Column A	Column B
d	1. reflecting telescope	a) gathers and amplifies radio waves from outer space
c	2. refracting telescope	b) made first practical use of the telescope
a	3. radio telescope	c) lens gathers light
e	4. Lippershey	d) mirror gathers light
b	5. Galileo	e) invented the optical telescope

REACHING OUT

Galileo made a large number of astronomical discoveries. Why was he able to do this?

Accept all logical responses. Likely responses include that Galileo's telescope allowed

him to see things that astronomers had not been able to see before.

SCIENCE *EXTRA*

Hubble Trouble

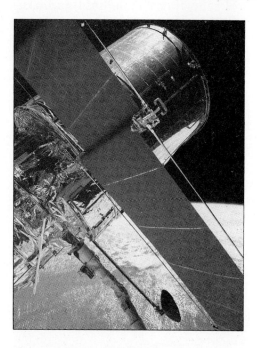

On April 24, 1990, the Space Shuttle *Discovery* lifted off with the Hubble Space Telescope (HST).

On Earth, telescopes must peer through the atmosphere, which can dim and blur images. The HST was designed to peer into space above Earth's atmosphere. There, HST would be able to see things that could not be seen from the ground. The telescope took years to build and cost 1.6 billion dollars.

During the first few months the HST was in orbit, the telescope's systems were all tested. These tests revealed a horrible and unexpected problem. Images from the telescope were very blurred!

The scientists ran a number of tests to figure out what the problem was. It turned out that the largest mirror in the telescope was the wrong shape.

Making a telescope mirror is a long and complex process. Very complicated devices are used to make sure that the mirror is ground into the proper shape.

When the largest mirror of the HST was made, the main testing device was not working correctly. The mirror was ground into the wrong shape. Tests using other devices hinted that there was something wrong with the mirror. However, the scientists making the mirror assumed that the main testing device was okay and that the other devices were wrong. Even scientists make mistakes.

Now that they know that the mirror is not the right shape, scientists are working on plans to fix the telescope. In 1993, astronauts from the Space Shuttle will repair it.

In addition to the largest mirror, the HST has other smaller mirrors and lenses in it. New mirrors will be made to replace these smaller mirrors in the HST. These new mirrors will be shaped to correct the problems with the main mirror, the way that eye glasses correct blurry vision. These new mirrors and lenses should make the telescope work almost as well as it was designed to.

Meanwhile, some of the experiments the HST was designed to do can still be done with its blurry vision. These experiments will be done until the telescope is repaired. Thus, the situation of the Hubble Space Telescope shows both the capabilities and the limitations of scientists.

What is a spectroscope? 3

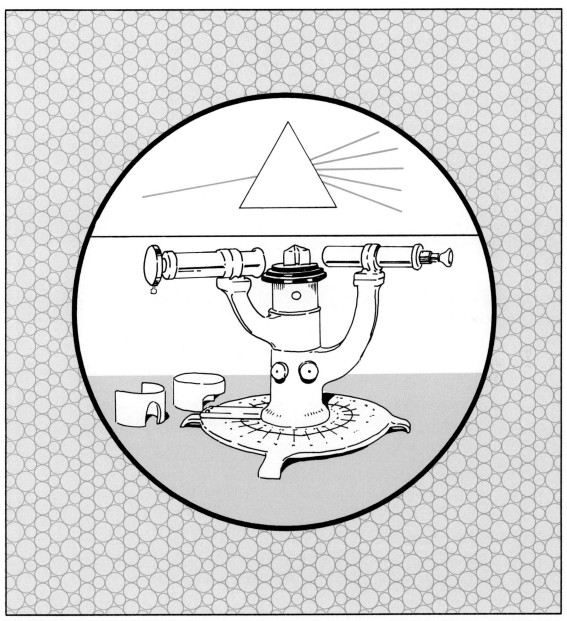

spectroscope [SPEK-truh-skohp]:   an instrument used to study the light coming from an object
spectrum: bands of different colors of light

LESSON 3 | What is a spectroscope?

Our sun is a star. Everyone knows this now But the early scientists did not believe this. There was no proof! The key to the proof came in 1850 with the invention of the **spectroscope** [SPEK-truh-scohp].

A spectroscope identifies elements by the colors they give off.

Every substance gives off light when it becomes hot enough. Every element gives off its own special color. A spectroscope separates the light into colored lines. We call these lines a **spectrum**. A spectrum is like a fingerprint. No two people have the same fingerprints. And, no two elements have the same spectrum. But the spectrum is always the same for a particular element.

For example:

This is what a sodium spectrum looks like.

yellow bands

Only sodium looks like this. No other elements looks exactly like this.

This is what a boron spectrum looks like.

green bands

Only boron looks like this. No other element looks exactly like this.

There are about 90 natural elements. We know the spectrum for each one. About 67 of them have been found in sunlight. This means that the sun contains at leasts 67 elements that are found on earth.

How do we know that the sun is a star? Simple! The spectroscope patterns of the sun and the stars are very similar.

UNDERSTANDING THE SPECTROSCOPE

The most important part of a spectroscope is a prism. A prism is glass shaped like a wedge. A prism can break up white light into a rainbow of colors.

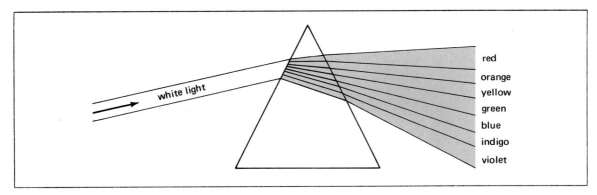

Figure A *Spectrum of white light.*

HOW A SPECTROSCOPE WORKS

Figure B *Spectroscope*

In a spectroscope, a prism breaks up the spectrums of individual substances.

1. The substance to be tested is placed in a flame. The flame is in line with the narrow slit of the spectroscope.

2. Light from the heated substance enters the slit.

3. The light passes through the prism.

4. The prism "breaks up" the light. A particular spectrum is formed.

5. The spectrum passes through the eyepiece into the eye of the viewer. The observer identified the spectrum.

Figure C

How is a spectroscope used to study light from objects in space? Figure C shows how.

1. The spectroscope is connected to the telescope.

2. A camera is connected to the spectroscope.

3. The camera photographs the spectrum.

4. Astronomers study and identify the spectrum.

The spectroscope does more than identify the chemical make up of the sun and the stars. We can use the spectroscope to figure out:

- the makeup of the atmosphere of planets
- how fast a heavenly body moves
- in what direction a heavenly body moves
- how hot a star is
- if a star is rotating
- if a star has a magnetic field

Figure D shows the spectrums of 9 elements. The numbers stand for different wavelengths (colors).

Figure D

Figure E

Figure E shows five spectrums coming from a heavenly body. Use Figure D to find out which element is shown by each spectrum. Write your answers below.

1. Spectrum 1: _____hydrogen_____

2. Spectrum 2: _____lithium_____

3. Spectrum 3: _____calcium_____

4. Spectrum 4: _____helium_____

5. Spectrum 5: _____barium_____

MATCHING

Match each term in Column A with its description in Column B. Write the correct letter in the space provided.

	Column A	**Column B**
e	1. astronomy	a) key part of a spectroscope
d	2. optical telescope	b) band of colors
c	3. spectroscope	c) analyzes light
a	4. prism	d) magnifies an image
b	5. spectrum	e) study of the heavens

How do astronomers measure distances?

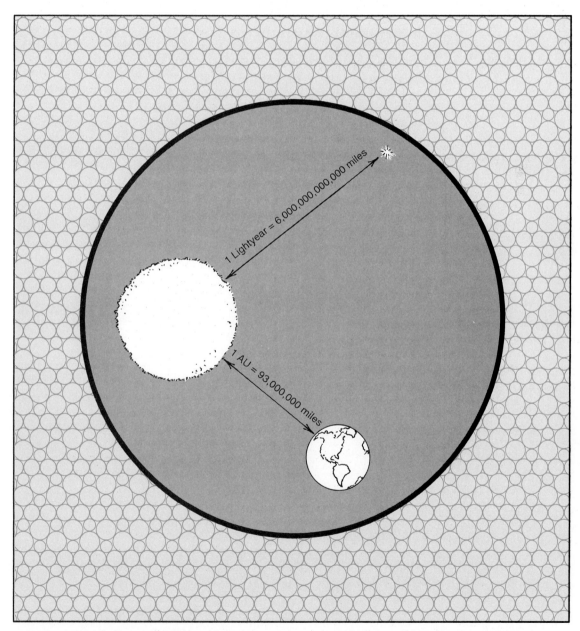

astronomical [as-truh-NOM-ih-kul] **unit:**   distance between the Earth and Sun; 150,000,000 kilometers

light-year: the distance that light travels in one year

LESSON 4 | How do astronomers measure distances?

How far away from school do you live? A few miles, maybe? How thick is this book? A centimeter or so. You use different measurements all the time. The unit you use (centimeters, meters, kilometers, miles) depends upon what you are measuring.

The distances measured by astronomers are big. VERY BIG. Astronomers have special units they use to measure distances.

Our sun is far away — about 150 million kilometers away.

Think of it! You would need to fly around the earth more than 1800 times to go that distance.

Astronomers call the distance to the sun an **astronomical** [as-truh-NOM-ih-kul] **unit** (AU). So one AU equals about 150,000,000 kilometers. Jupiter is 778,300,000 kilometers away or a little more than 5 AU away from the sun. So Jupiter is about 5 times as far from the sun as Earth is. It is much easier to use AUs than kilometers.

An AU is very large. However, the distances between stars are even larger. Much larger. The closest star to the sun is about 42,000,000,000,000 kilometers away. That is 282,000 AU, and that is the closest star. Other stars are much farther. Some stars are so far away that even AU's are too small. The distances between stars are measured in light-years. What is a light-year?

A **light-year** is the distance that light travels in one year.

Let's see what this means.

- Light travels about 300,000 kilometers (186,000 miles) every second.

- There are 31,536,000 seconds in a year.

- If you multiply the seconds in a year by the speed of light, you find out how far light travels in one year.

How far is it? Nearly 10 trillion (10,000,000,000,000) kilometers (6 trillion miles). This one light-year.

10 trillion kilometers! Wow! That's equal to 125 million trips around the world.

The table below shows how far away the planets are form the sun.

Planet	Astronomical Units	Kilometers
Mercury	0.4	58,000,000
Venus	0.7	108,000,000
Earth	1.0	150,000,000
Mars	1.5	230,000,000
Jupiter	5.2	778,000,000
Saturn	9.5	1,427,000,000
Uranus	19.2	2,870,000,000
Neptune	30.1	4,500,000,000
Pluto	39.4	5,900,000,000

To travel the distance between the sun and Pluto, you would have to circle the Earth **more than 460,000 times!**

HOW FAR AWAY ARE THE STARS

Figure A

The closest star to Earth (other than the sun) is 4.3 light-years away.

That's **423,000,000,000,000** kilometers or **267,000,000,000,000** miles.

Now here is something to think about. Most other stars are millions and hundreds of millions of light-years away! In fact, some stars in distance galaxies are believed to be about 16 million light years away.

That's **16,000,000,000,000,000,000,000,000** kilometers or **9,600,000,000000,000000,000** miles.

FILL IN THE BLANK

Complete each statement using a term or terms from the list below. Write your answers in the spaces provided.

150,000,000	ten trillion	light
star	300,000	second
one year	light-year	stars
kilometers	sun	astronomical units
Earth		

1. The sun is a _____star_____ .

2. The sun is _____150,000,000_____ kilometers from Earth.

3. Distances between planets are measured in ___astronomical units___ .

4. One astronomical unit (AU) is the distance between _____Earth_____ and

   the _____sun_____ .

5. All the other _____stars_____ are much farther away from Earth than the sun is.

6. We do not measure the distances between stars in _____kilometers_____ .

7. The distances between stars are measured in a unit called the

   _____light-year_____ .

8. A light-year is the distance that_____light_____ travels in _____one year_____ .

9. Light travels _____300,000_____ kilometers per _____second_____ .

10. One light-year is equal to about_____ten trillion_____ kilometers.

REACHING OUT

People sometimes say that when we look at stars that are very far away that we are

"looking back in time." Why do people say this? _____Accept all logical responses._____

Likely responses include that light we see from a star was given off by the star a long

time ago. We are seeing the way the star was a long time ago.

What is parallax?

5

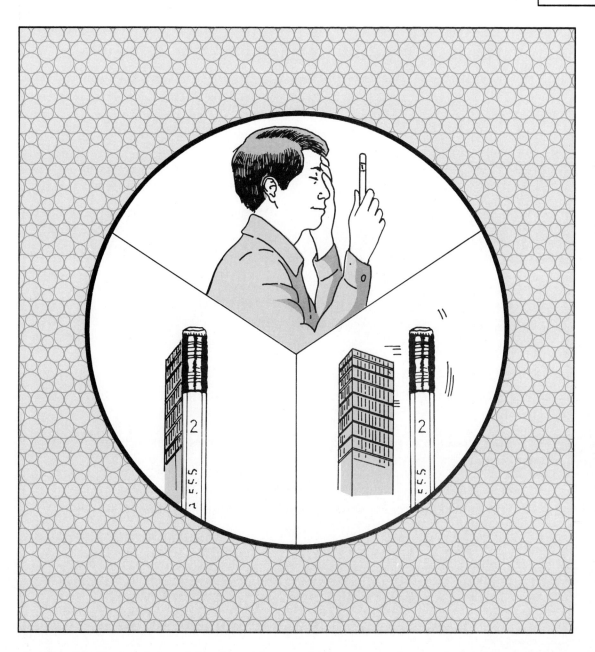

parallax [PAR-uh-laks]:   shift of position an object seems to have when it is seen from two
 different points

LESSON 5 | What is parallax?

Any object seems to shift position when it is viewed from two different points. We call this apparent shift in position **parallax** [PAR-uh-laks]. You can see parallax while sitting at your desk. Do this:

1. Hold one finger a short distance in front of your face.

2. Close your right eye.

3. Now open your right eye and close your left eye.

4. Repeat this several times.

Your finger did not move. But it seemed to. It seemed to move back and forth compared to the background. It is this apparent shift that we call parallax.

Parallax lets us measure the distances to many stars. It even helps us measure the size of the sun, moon, and planets.

Some stars are so far away that scientists cannot use parallax to figure out how far away they are. Scientists use other methods to try to determine how far away these stars are.

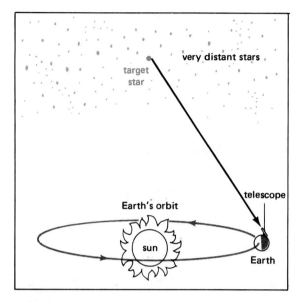

Figure A

Step 1 A nearby "target" star is chosen. Distance stars are in the background. They are photographed together.

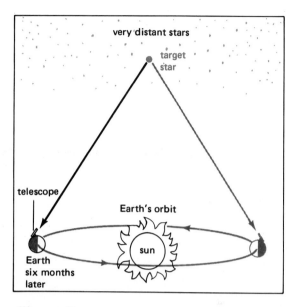

Figure B

Step 2 A second photograph is made six months later. The earth is then exactly at the opposite end of its path around the sun.

Figure C *The first photo*

Figure D *The photo taken six months later*

Compare the photos. Notice that the target star is not in the same spot. It seems to have shifted compared to the reference stars. Astronomers measure the angle the target star seems to have shifted. This angle is called the angle of greatest shift.

The final step is simple math. A tri-angle is set up as in Figure E.

The base is the distance between the earth's position six months apart. This distance is known.

The angle of greatest shift lets us find angles a and b.

With these figures, we can find the distance to the target star.

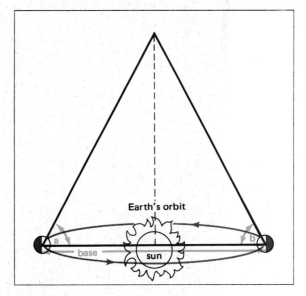

Figure E

FILL IN THE BLANK

Complete each statement using a term or terms from the list below. Write your answers in the spaces provided. Some words may be used more than once.

distances	halfway	shift position	kilometers
two	parallax	light-years	six months

1. Every object seems to __shift position__ when seen from two different places.

2. This apparent shift in position is called __parallax__ .

3. Parallax allows us to measure the __distances__ to some objects in space.

4. Parallax can be used to measure __distances__ to the sun, moon, and planets.

5. To measure the distance to a star, at least __two__ observations are needed.

6. For the best results, the second observation is made exactly __six months__ after the first.

7. In six months the earth has traveled __halfway__ through its path around the sun.

8. The distances between stars is measured in __light years__ , not in __kilometers__ .

How does a rocket move? $\boxed{6}$

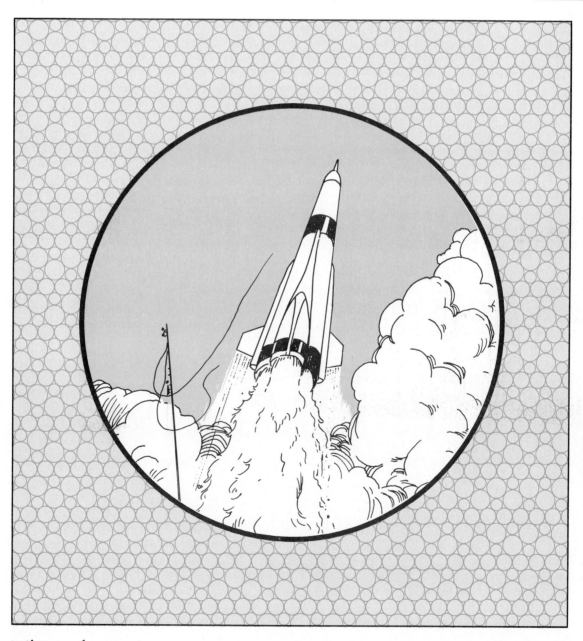

action: a force
reaction: an opposing force that balances an action

LESSON 6 | How does a rocket move?

Did you ever blow up a balloon and let go suddenly? What happened? It flew through the air. It zigzagged a bit. But generally, it flew in the direction <u>opposite</u> to the mouthpiece.

The balloon acted like a small rocket. It moved forward as the air was escaping from the mouthpiece.

Huge rockets have lifted astronauts into space. Smaller rockets have placed satellites into orbit around the earth. Large or small, all rockets work on the same idea—even your balloon "rocket."

What is this idea?

You have heard of Isaac Newton. He explained gravity and inertia. Newton also helped explain how a rocket moves. It is explained in Newton's *Third Law of Motion*. This law says that every time there is a force acting upon an object in one direction there is an equally strong force acting in the opposite direction.

- The first force is called the **action**.

- The opposite force is called the **reaction**.

The scientific way to state Newton's *Third Law of Motion* is:

For every action, there is an equal reaction in the opposite direction.

In a rocket, the action pushes downward. This force comes from fuel burning in the rocket's engines. You have probably seen films of flames shooting downward during a blastoff. As the hot gases move downward, the rocket moves upward into the sky . . . And away it goes!

A balloon can move like a rocket. Figures A and B show two blown-up balloons.

• The mouthpiece of the balloon in Figure A is closed.

• The mouthpiece of the balloon in Figure B has just been opened.

Look at the figures.

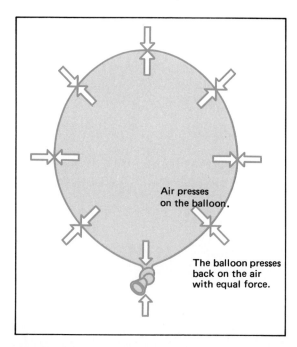

Air presses
on the balloon.

The balloon presses
back on the air
with equal force.

Figure A

Answer these questions about the balloon in Figure A.

1. The forces _____are_____

   are, are not

   balanced.

2. The balloon _____will not_____

   will, will not

   move forward.

3. Does a closed blown-up balloon

   move like a rocket? _____no_____

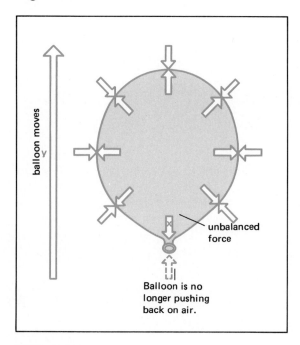

balloon moves

y

unbalanced
force

Balloon is no
longer pushing
back on air.

Figure B

Answer these questions about the balloon in Figure B.

4. The forces are _____no longer_____

   still, no longer

   balanced.

5. Some air is escaping from

   _____x_____ .

   x, y

6. As the air escapes, it causes the balloon to move in the direction of

   _____y_____ .

   x y

29

Figure C

Figure C shows a rocket. Study Figure C. Answer the questions.

7. A rocket carries fuel. What else does a rocket carry? _____oxygen_____

Oxygen helps the fuel to burn.

8. **a)** Does an airplane carry its own oxygen? _____no_____

   b) Why does a rocket carry its own oxygen? __The rocket goes into__ __space where there is no oxygen.__

9. Hot gases escape through the _____exhaust nozzles_____ .

10. Arrow——B——— stands
    A, B

    for the action.

11. Arrow——A——— stands
    A, B

    for the reaction.

12. Arrow_____A_____ points
    A, B

    in the direction the rocket is moving.

MATCHING

Match each term in Column A with its description in Column B. Write the correct letter in the space provided.

	Column A		Column B
__c__	**1.** an action	**a)**	how actions and reactions are related
__a__	**2.** opposite	**b)**	needed for a fuel to burn
__e__	**3.** fuel	**c)**	causes a reaction
__b__	**4.** oxygen	**d)**	wrote the *Third Law of Motion*
__d__	**5.** Isaac Newton	**e)**	burns

THE SATURN V

The Saturn V rocket was America's most powerful rocket. This rocket took astronauts to the moon.

Here are some interesting facts about the Saturn V:

- The Saturn V stands 111 meters (364 feet) tall. This is 18 meters (59 feet) taller than the Statue of Liberty.

- At lift-off, it uses 13.6 metric tons (15 tons) of fuel every second. This is enough fuel to run a family car for nearly 5 years.

- Its lift-off mass is 2,721,5543 kilograms (about 6,000,000 pounds). This is equal to the mass of 20 loaded airliners—or 1,818 medium-sized cars.

Figure D

EXPERIENCES WITH ACTIONS AND REACTIONS

Look at Figures E through H. Each figure shows an action and a reaction.

Identify the action and reaction in each picture. Answer by letter.

Figure E

1. Action ———— b ————

   Reaction ———— a ————

Figure F

2. Action ———— d ————

   Reaction ———— c ————

Figure G

3. Action _____e_____

   Reaction _____f_____

Figure H

4. Action _____g_____

   Reaction _____h_____

FILL IN THE BLANK

Complete each statement using a term or terms from the list below. Write your answers in the spaces provided.

Saturn V	left	Isaac Newton
fuel	down	opposite
action	reaction	oxygen

1. The scientist who stated the *Third Law of Motion* was _____Isaac Newton_____ .

2. Newton's *Third Law of Motion* states that every _____action_____ has an equal _____reaction_____ .

3. Actions and reactions are _____opposite_____ in direction.

4. If the direction of an action is up, then the direction of a reaction is _____down_____ .

5. If the direction of an action is to the right, then the direction of a reaction is to the _____left_____ .

6. Rockets sent into space carry _____oxygen_____ and _____fuel_____ .

7. America's most powerful rocket was the _____Saturn V_____ .

What are satellites and space probes?

7

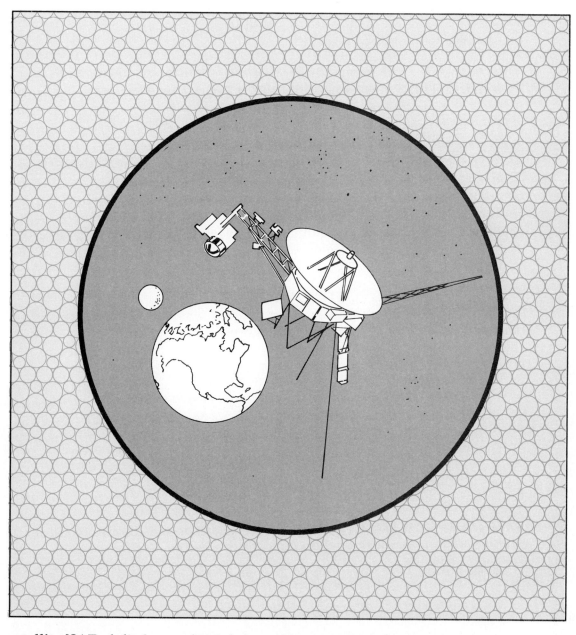

satellite [SAT-uh-lite]:   an object that revolves around another object
space probe: a machine that is sent from Earth to study other objects in space

LESSON 7 | What are satellites and space probes?

The moon is a satellite of the earth. A **satellite** [SAT-uh-lite] is something that orbits another object in space.

On October 4, 1957, the Soviet Union launched Sputnik into orbit around the earth. Sputnik became the earth's first artificial satellite.

Since Sputnik, hundreds of satellites have been launched. Satellites perform all sorts of functions. There are four basic types of satellites.

EARTH SENSING SATELLITES   These satellites have cameras or some other kind of sensors pointed down at the earth. As the satellite flies over different places, the sensors on the satellite study these places. Satellites are very helpful in the study of isolated places that are hard for people to get to, such as the tops of mountains. Earth sensing satellites also are used by the military of some countries to study what is going on in other countries.

SPACE SENSING SATELLITES   We need the earth's atmosphere to survive, but the atmosphere often is in the way when we try to study things in space. Satellites are often put in orbit above the earth's atmosphere. These satellites have a clear view of what scientists want to study in space.

COMMUNICATION SATELLITES   Radio waves cannot travel through the ground, and the curvature of the earth gets in the way of radio signals that are sent far across the planet. Instead, radio signals are sent to satellites in space. The satellites, in turn, send the signal to another place on the earth. In fact, sometimes a satellite sends a message on to another satellite which then sends it to the ground. Messages can be sent all the way around the world this way.

NAVIGATION SATELLITES   Ships, planes, and even cars can pinpoint their location on the earth by "listening" to the signals sent by several navigation satellites.

Figure A   *The TIROS weather satellite helps weathermen make their forecasts.*

Figure B   *The Solar Maximum satellite studies the sun from space.*

Figure C   *The Intelsat satellite relays telephone calls and television programs.*

Figure D   *The Navstar satellite helps ships, aircraft and land vehicles navigate.*

In studying planets and other objects in the solar system, sometimes there is no substitute for "being there." However, it would be very expensive, and very dangerous, to send people to other planets. Instead, scientists send robots similar to satellites toward these objects. These robots are called space probes.

Space probes come in all shapes and sizes and can perform various functions. Most space probes have cameras of some type to take pictures of the objects they are studying. Because space probes are much closer to the objects they are studying, they can take much better pictures than we can from Earth. *Voyager 1* and *Voyager 2* are two space probes that flew by Jupiter, Saturn, Uranus, and Neptune.

Figure E *Voyager*

Some space probes are designed to land on other planets. These probes can then study the surface of the planet. *Viking 1* and *Viking 2* were two probes that landed on Mars in 1976.

Figure F *Viking*

TRUE OR FALSE

In the space provided, write "true" if the sentence is true. Write "false" if the sentence is false.

False	**1.**	Sputnik was the earth's first satellite.
True	**2.**	Sputnik was the earth's first artificial satellite.
True	**3.**	The earth has one natural satellite.
False	**4.**	The earth has no natural satellites.
True	**5.**	Satellites can be used to study the earth.
True	**6.**	Satellites can be used to study space.
False	**7.**	Space probes carry people to other planets.
True	**8.**	Space probes study objects in space.
False	**9.**	Space probes cannot land on planets.
False	**10.**	*Voyager 1* and *Voyager 2* studied Mars.

MATCHING

Match each term in Column A with its description in Column B. Write the correct letter in the space provided.

Column A

e	**1.** navigation satellites
b	**2.** earth sensing satellites
a	**3.** space sensing satellites
d	**4.** communication satellites
c	**5.** space probes

Column B

a) used to study other objects in space from earth orbit

b) weather satellites

c) *Voyager 1* and *Voyager 2*

d) relay telephone calls and television programs

e) help ships, planes, and cars find their way

WORD SEARCH

The list on the left contains words that you have used in this Lesson. Find and circle each word where it appears in the box. The spellings may go in any direction: up, down, left, right, or diagonally.

SATELLITE
NAVIGATION
ROCKET
VOYAGER
VIKING
COMMUNICATION
NEWTON
EARTH
SPACE
MARS

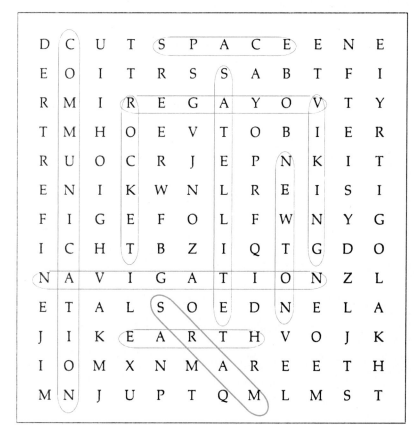

REACHING OUT

Why is it cheaper to send space probes to other planets instead of sending people?

Accept all logical responses. Likely responses include that people need life support equipment that is expensive. Also, if people went on trips to other planets, the spacecraft would have to return the people to Earth. Space probes only have to go one way.

What is a space shuttle? 8

space shuttle: reusable space vehicle

LESSON 8 | What is a space shuttle?

Imagine that your family owned a car that could be used JUST ONCE. After only one trip — long or short, it had to be junked. Sounds ridiculous? It certainly does! But this is precisely how the space program operated until April 12, 1981. On that date, Columbia, America's first Space Shuttle was launched. It went into orbit — and then returned to earth.

A **Space Shuttle** is a reusable space vehicle. Until the Shuttle, no part of a space launch (that blasted off) was reused. Some parts fell into the ocean. Others burned up while returning to Earth. Even the capsules that carried astronauts were not reused.

This approach to space exploration was too expensive. Scientists knew this. They wanted a cheaper way to send things into space, so they developed the Space Shuttle.

The Space Shuttle is designed to be used over and over again. Only one part — its main fuel tank must be replaced.

A Space Shuttle system has three main parts:

- the Shuttle orbiter itself, with its three main engines
- two solid rocket boosters (for extra thrust)
- external tank (a large fuel tank)

1. At blastoff, all parts are connected. The main engines and the boosters both burn with a deafening roar. The Shuttle lifts off and heads towards space.

2. After a few minutes, the boosters have used up their fuel. They separate and parachute back to earth. They are recovered and re-used. The main fuel tank is still attached and continues to feed the main engines.

3. When the Shuttle reaches its proper speed and position, the main fuel tank breaks away. It burns up as it plunges back through the atmosphere. This is the only part that is not reused.

4. The Shuttle is now in orbit around the Earth. It may continue in orbit for several days. While in orbit, the crew carries out their mission.

5. Its mission completed, the Shuttle returns to earth. Since it has no fuel, it glides back to earth.

6. The Shuttle lands on wheels, like an airplane. It is then made ready to be reused.

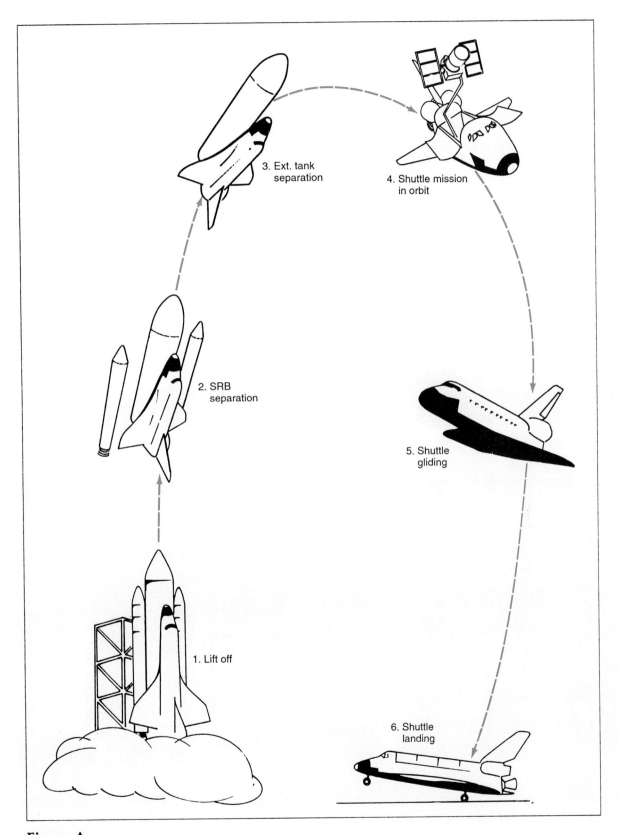

Figure A

The Space Shuttle can do a number of things. In fact, the Shuttle is so useful that it sometimes has been called a "space truck." The figures below show some of the things the Shuttle can do.

Figure B *Carry people into space*

Figure C *Carry satellites and space probes*

Figure D *Return objects from space to Earth*

Figure E *Perform experiments in zero gravity*

Figure F *Study Earth from space*

Figure G *Build and supply a space station*

TRUE OR FALSE

In the space provided, write "true" if the sentence is true. Write "false" if the sentence is false.

True	**1.**	The Shuttle has two solid rocket boosters.
False	**2.**	The external tank is carried into space.
True	**3.**	The external tank is not reusable.
False	**4.**	The Shuttle only carries people into space.
True	**5.**	The Shuttle has a large cargo bay to carry things into space.
False	**6.**	The Shuttle lands on water.
True	**7.**	The Shuttle lands like an airplane.
False	**8.**	The Shuttle takes off like an airplane.
True	**9.**	The Shuttle takes off like a rocket.
True	**10.**	The Shuttle can bring satellites back to Earth.

FILL IN THE BLANK

Complete each statement using a term or terms from the list below. Write your answers in the spaces provided. Some words may be used more than once.

launch   external tank   solid rocket boosters
orbits   shuttle orbiter   joined
Space Shuttle   repair   glides
wheels   is not

1. The <u>Space Shuttle</u> is the first reusable spacecraft.

2. The main parts of a Shuttle system are the <u>shuttle orbiter</u> , two <u>solid rocket boosters</u> and an <u>external tank</u> .

3. Extra upward thrust is supplied by the <u>solid rocket boosters</u> .

4. At lift-off, all the parts of the Shuttle system are <u>joined</u> .

5. The first parts of the Shuttle system to separate, are the <u>solid rocket boosters</u> .

6. The external tank <u>is not</u> reused.

7. The shuttle <u>orbits</u> Earth.

8. Not only can the Shuttle be used to <u>launch</u> satellites, it can be used to <u>repair</u> them.

9. When its mission is completed, the Shuttle <u>glides</u> back to earth.

10. The Shuttle lands on <u>wheels</u> like a regular airplane.

REACHING OUT

Will the Shuttle last forever? Why or why not? <u>Accept all logical responses. Likely responses include that the Shuttle will not last forever because its parts wear out. Eventually all of the parts will stop working.</u>

How do humans survive in space?

9

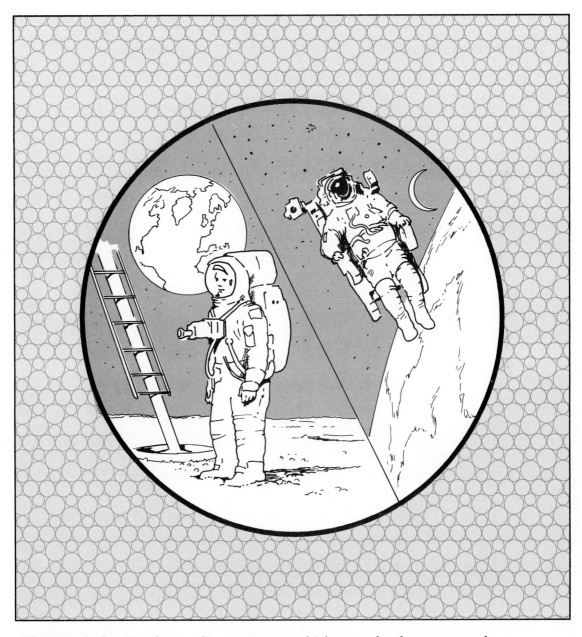

dehydrated [dee-HY-drayt-ed]:   an item in which water has been removed
environment [in-VY-run-munt]:   the surroundings that living things live in

LESSON 9 | How do humans survive in space?

Everything that surrounds an organism is called its **environment.** Air and water are parts of the environment. So are the temperature, air pressure, and food.

Our environment is well suited for life. We have air to breathe, food to eat, and water to drink. The air pressure is just right. In most places the temperature is never too hot or too cold. The atmosphere blocks out harmful radiation. In short, we live in a "friendly" environment.

The environment in space, however, is not friendly to humans. It presents many problems. You could not live in space the same way that you live on earth. There is no air to breathe. There is also no air pressure. The temperature is either much too hot or much too cold. No food grows in space. And there is nothing to block out harmful radiation.

There are other problems too. Living things produce wastes. The wastes must be eliminated. On earth, we have no problem eliminating our wastes. Every time we breathe out we release carbon dioxide into the air. Heat and moisture from our skin goes into the air, too. We use water to flush away the liquid and solid wastes we produce.

In space, getting rid of wastes is not so easy. In fact, just keeping clean is a problem.

On earth, gravity holds you to the ground. In a moving spacecraft, there is no gravity. Actually, gravity from outer space does pull upon the spacecraft. But the movement of the spacecraft cancels it out. The result is "zero" gravity. In zero gravity a person seems to weigh nothing. Just imagine. You would float around the spacecraft if you didn't hold onto something!

Because of all these problems of living in space, astronauts must bring along their own environment! It must be like the environment found on earth. Special clothing and instruments have been designed so that the traveler in space has everything that is needed to stay alive.

Figure D

Figure E

Very little can be done about weightlessness. Astronauts prepare themselves for this funny feeling. Airplanes can be piloted to mimic zero gravity. Astronauts also practice missions underwater. In this way an astronaut learns what to expect.

1. Do the astronauts feel the pull of gravity in a moving spacecraft? _____no_____

2. How much do the astronauts seem to weigh there? _____nothing_____

3. How do astronauts prepare for the feeling of weightlessness? __They train on__ airplanes and under water. _____

4. How is being in water like being in space? __You can "float" in both places.__

FILL IN THE BLANK

Complete each statement using a term or terms from the list below. Write your answers in the spaces provided.

temperature	airplanes	oxygen
spacecraft	earth	under water

1. A _____spacecraft_____ must supply everything an astronaut needs.

2. The _____temperature_____ in a spacecraft is kept at a comfortable level.

3. The pressure in a spacecraft is like the pressure on the _____earth_____ .

4. Living things need _____oxygen_____ to survive.

5. Astronauts train for weightlessness on _____airplanes_____ and _____underwater_____.

MATCHING

Match each term in Column A with its description in Column B. Write the correct letter in the space provided.

Column A		Column B
__e__	1. carbon dioxide	a) copies zero gravity
__d__	2. shields	b) needed for life
__a__	3. airplane	c) carries everything the astronaut needs
__c__	4. space suit	d) block radiation
__b__	5. oxygen	e) waste gas

REACHING OUT

Spacesuits are white. There is a good reason for this. What is this reason?

White reflects light more than other colors.

_____

_____

50

What are the earth's motions?

revolution [reh-vuh-LOO-shun]:   the traveling of an object around another object
rotation [roh-TAY-shun]:   the spinning of an object on its axis

LESSON 10 | What are the earth's motions?

Find a quiet place where you can be alone for a few minutes. It can be anywhere—in your room, your yard, a park, or vacant lot or field. Just as long as you can look around and observe what's happening.

What is happening? If your answer is "nothing," think again. In the minute or so that you have been looking around, the spot you are standing on has <u>moved</u>. It has traveled a distance of about 17 kilometers (10 miles)! In 24 hours, that same spot will have traveled a circular distance of more than 25,000 kilometers (15,000 miles)!

And that's not all. While you are looking around, you are traveling through space. You are moving at a speed of about 30 kilometers (18 miles) per second!

How can this be? How can you be moving and not feel it? Or see it? The reason you can't sense the motion is because <u>everything</u> around you is moving too. Your home, the trees, the air and clouds—everything is moving at the same speed.

Actually, the entire earth is moving. In fact, there are two different motions of the earth. Both are happening at the same time.

First, the earth is "spinning like a top." It is turning, or rotating, on its axis. This motion is called **rotation** [roh-TAY-shun]. It takes the earth 24 hours to complete one rotation. This time period is called a day.

Second, the earth is moving through space. It is traveling, or revolving, around the sun. This motion is called **revolution** [reh-vuh-LOO-shun]. The earth completes one revolution in 365 1/4 days. This time period is called a year.

THE EARTH'S ROTATION

You cannot feel it, but the earth is spinning on its axis. It rotates from west to east. You may think, "So what? If I cannot feel it spinning, what difference does it make?"

Let's take a quick look at the "difference" rotation makes.

Figure A

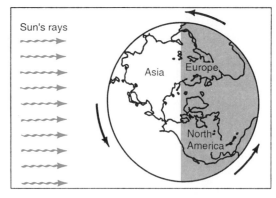

Figure B

The Sun's rays can only shine on one side of the Earth at a time. It is daytime in the half of the Earth that gets the light and nighttime in the half of the Earth that does not get the light. As the Earth rotates the part of the Earth that the sun shines on **changes**. Every part of the Earth has daytime, then night time, then daytime again.

THE EARTH'S REVOLUTION

In one year, the earth travels about 940,000,000 kilometers! It *revolves* around the sun. You can't feel this motion either. But there are ways to tell the earth revolves. Look at Figure C.

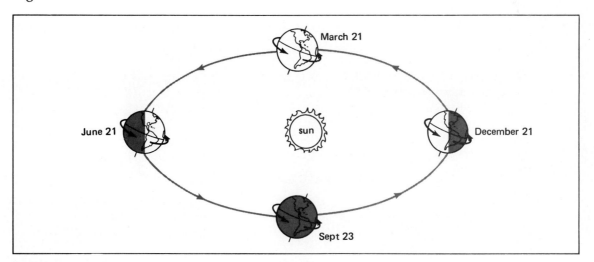

Figure C

The drawing shows the earth at different points in its trip around the sun. Notice the dates. At each of these dates, we start a different season. The earth's revolution (along with the tilt of its axis) causes the seasons.

ROTATION OR REVOLUTION?

Each statement describes something caused by one of the earth's motions. Beside each statement, write the word "rotation" or "revolution."

1. The sun sets in the west. _____ rotation _____

2. The "big dipper" moves across the sky. _____ rotation _____

3. The leaves turn from green to red. _____ revolution _____

4. The sun is right overhead at noon. _____ rotation _____

5. Flowers burst into bloom. _____ revolution _____

REACHING OUT

Look at the two figures below. Beneath each figure, tell whether it shows **rotation or revolution.** Explain your answer.

Figure D

The race cars show rotation. They are traveling around a track.

Figure E

The skater shows rotation. She is moving (spinning) on a central point (the skates).

What causes day and night?

11

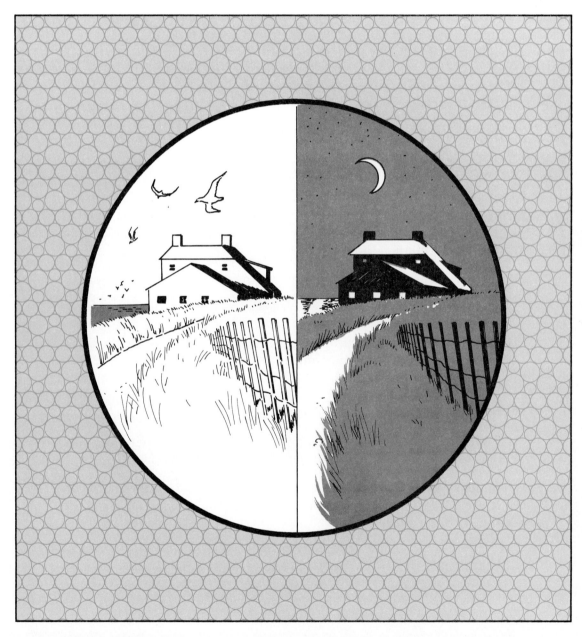

equinox [EE-kwuh-nahks]:   day on which the sun shines directly on the equator
Northern Hemisphere: the part of the earth north of the equator
solstice [SAHL-stis]:   day on which the North Pole points toward or away from the sun
Southern Hemisphere: the part of the earth south of the equator

LESSON 11 | What causes day and night?

Usually when you go to sleep, it is dark. You wake up the next morning, and it is light. Several hours will pass and day will change to night again.

What causes day and night? The changes of day and night are caused by the earth's rotation.

As the earth rotates, only one half faces the sun at any given time. The half that is facing the sun has day. The opposite side (the side that is facing away from the sun) has night.

As the earth rotates, new parts face the sun. Places that have night slowly turn to day. One complete rotation of the earth takes 24 hours. In most places, therefore, one change from night to day and then back to night again takes 24 hours.

How many of these 24 hours are night? How many are day? It depends upon two things: the time of year, and how far from the equator a place is.

If the earth's axis were vertical (straight up and down), all parts of the earth would have 12 hours day and 12 hours night all year-round. But, the earth's axis is not vertical. The earth's axis is tilted 23 1/2 degrees.

As the earth moves around the sun, the tilt of the earth does not change. The earth just changes its position compared to the sun. Sometimes the earth is tilted so that the northern portion of the earth is facing the sun. This makes the days longer than nights in the **Northern Hemisphere.**

When the earth moves to the other side of the sun, the southern portion of the earth is facing the sun. Now the days are longer than nights in the **Southern Hemisphere.**

How far north and south of the equator a place is, also affects how long day and night will be. The farther north or south of the equator a place is, the greater the difference in length there is between day and night.

Study Figure A. Then answer the questions or fill in the blanks.

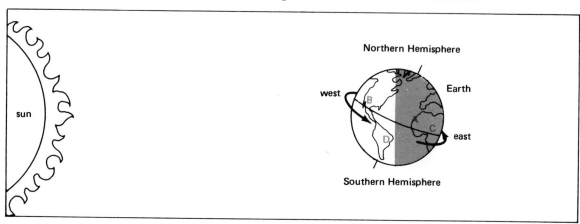

Figure A

1. The earth turns on its axis. Another way of saying this is the earth

   _____rotates_____ on its axis.
   revolves, rotates

2. How many hours does one rotation of earth take? _____24_____

3. At any given time,

   a) how much of the earth is facing the sun?_____one-half_____

   b) how much of the sun is facing away from the sun? _____one-half_____

4. The part of the earth facing the sun has_____day_____ .
   night, day

5. The part of the earth facing away from the sun has _____night_____ .
   night, day

6. The earth rotates from _____west to east_____ .
   east to west, west to east

A, B, C, and D are places on the earth.

7. **a)** Which of these places are having day? _____B and D_____

   b) Which of these places are having night? _____A and C_____

8. Of the places that are having day, which one will move into night first?_____D_____

9. Of the places that are having night, which one will move into day first?_____C_____

10. **a)** Which places are in the Northern Hemisphere? _____B, A, and C_____

    b) Which place is in the Southern Hemisphere?_____D_____

Study Figure B. Answer the questions or fill in the blanks.

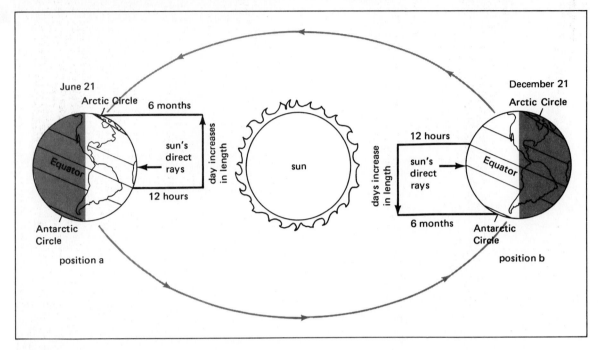

Figure B

Position a shows the earth on June 21.

Position b shows the earth six months later on December 21. It has now come halfway along its revolution around the earth.

1. Look at the earth's axis on both dates. Has the angle of its tilt compared to the sun

   changed? _____no_____

2. Has the direction of the tilt compared to the sun changed? _____yes_____

JUNE 21

On June 21, the North Pole points directly toward the sun. This day in the Northern Hemisphere is the summer **solstice** [SAHL-stis]. On this day the North Pole has 24 hours of sunlight.

1. On June 21, the _____Northern_____ Hemisphere tilts toward the sun.

Northern, Southern

2. On June 21, _____Southern_____ Hemisphere tilts away from the sun.

Northern, Southern

3. On June 21, the _____Northern_____ Hemisphere has more hours of sunlight.

Northern, Southern

4. On June 21, the _____Southern_____ Hemisphere has fewer hours of sunlight.

Northern, Southern

5. On June 21, days are longer in the _____Northern_____ Hemisphere.

   Northern, Southern

6. If days in the Northern Hemisphere are longer, then days in the Southern Hemisphere are _____shorter_____ .

   longer, shorter

7. On June 21, the _____equator_____ has 12 hours of day and 12 hours of night.

   equator, arctic circle, antarctic circle

8. As you move farther north, the days become _____longer_____ .

   longer, shorter

9. On June 21, there are _____24_____ hours of daylight in the Arctic circle.

   zero, 12, 24

10. When it is day at the Arctic Circle, it is_____night_____ at the Antarctic Circle.

DECEMBER 21

On December 21, the North Pole points away from the sun. This day in the Northern Hemisphere is the winter solstice. On this day, the North Pole has 24 hours of darkness.

1. On December 21, the _____Southern_____ Hemisphere leans toward the sun.

   Northern, Southern

2. On December 21, the _____Northern_____ Hemisphere leans away from the sun.

   Northern, Southern

3. On December 21, the _____Southern_____ Hemisphere has more hours of sunlight.

   Northern, Southern

4. On December 21, the _____Northern_____ Hemisphere has fewer hours of sunlight.

   Northern, Southern

5. On December 21, days are longer in the _____Southern_____ Hemisphere.

   Northern, Southern

6. If days in the Southern Hemisphere are longer, then days in the Northern Hemisphere are _____shorter_____ .

   longer, shorter

7. On December 21, the _____equator_____ has 12 hours of day and 12 hours of night.

   equator, arctic circle, antarctic circle

8. The length of day and night _____does not_____ seem to change at the equator.

   does, does not

9. On December 21, there are_____24_____ hours of daylight in the Antarctic Circle.

   zero, 12, 24

10. When it is day at the Antarctic Circle it is _____night_____ at the Arctic Circle.

EQUINOXES

For most of the year, the number of hours of day and night in the Northern and Southern Hemispheres are unequal.

On just two days of the year, every place on earth has an equal number of hours of day and night.

On March 21 and September 21, neither hemisphere leans towards the sun. On these days, every place on earth has 12 hours of daylight and 12 hours of darkness.

March 21 and September 21 are called **equinoxes** [EE-kwuh-nahks-ez].

Figure C shows the earth during one revolution around the sun. Study Figure C. Then answer the questions or fill in the blanks.

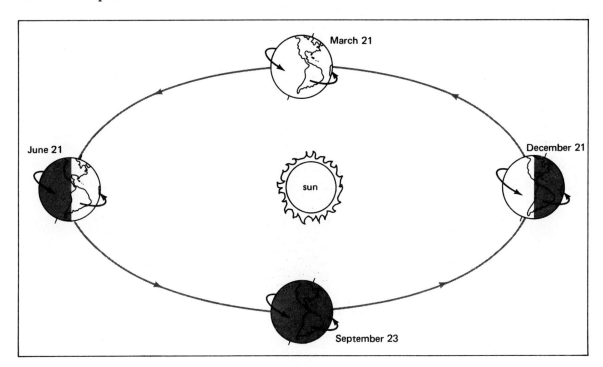

Figure C

1. The earth _____rotates_____ on its axis.
    rotates, revolves

2. The earth _____revolves_____ around the sun.
    rotates, revolves

3. One rotation makes one _____day_____.
    day, year

4. One revolution makes one _____year_____.
    day, year

5. Look at the earth's axis on each date.

    a) Has the angle changed? _____no_____

    b) Has the axis changed the way it leans toward or away from the sun? _____no_____

60

1. The Northern Hemisphere leans toward the sun most on _____June 21_____.

2. The Northern Hemisphere leans away from the sun most on _____December 21_____.

3. The earth's axis does not lean toward nor away from the sun on
    _____March 21_____ and _____September 21_____.

4. The longest day of the year in the Northern Hemisphere is _____June 21_____.

5. The shortest day of the year in the Northern Hemisphere is _____December 21_____.

6. Day and night are equal in length everywhere on earth on _____March 21_____
    and _____September 21_____.

7. In the Northern Hemisphere, between June 21 and September 21, days become

    _____shorter_____.
    longer, shorter

8. In the Northern Hemisphere, between September 21 and December 21, days become

    _____shorter_____.
    longer, shorter

9. In the Northern Hemisphere, between December 21 and March 21, days become

    _____longer_____.
    longer, shorter

10. In the Northern Hemisphere, between March 21 and June 21, days become

    _____longer_____.
    longer, shorter

11. Differences in the number of hours of day and night happen _____slowly_____.
    slowly, suddenly

12. In which hemisphere do you live? _____answers will vary_____

13. What is today's date? _____answers will vary_____

14. On this date, where you live, there will be more hours of _____answers will vary_____.
    day, night

15. Tomorrow, day will last a few minutes _____answers will vary_____ and night will last a few

    minutes _____answers will vary_____.
    longer, shorter

MATCHING

Match each term in Column A with its description in Column B. Write the correct letter in the space provided.

	Column A		**Column B**
__d__	**1.** earth's rotation	**a)**	tilt of earth's axis
__a__	**2.** 23 1/2°	**b)**	fewest hours of night in the Northern Hemisphere
__e__	**3.** December 21	**c)**	day and night equal everywhere
__b__	**4.** June 21	**d)**	causes day and night
__c__	**5.** March 21 and September 23	**e)**	most daylight hours in the Southern Hemisphere

REACHING OUT

What do we call these dates in the Northern Hemisphere? Write the names next to the dates.

December 21 __winter solstice__   March 21 __equinox (spring)__

September 21 __equinox (fall)__   June 21 __summer solstice__

What are time zones? | 12 |

prime meridian [muh-RID-ee-un]:   imaginary line that runs north and south through Greenwich, England

international date line: imaginary line that runs north and south and separates one day from the next

time zone: part of the earth where it is the same time; the earth has 24 time zones.

LESSON 12 | What are time zones?

When it is 12 noon in New York, it is three hours earlier, (9 A.M.) in California. At the same moment in Paris, France, it is five hours later (5 P.M.).

Why is the time different around the world?

Time depends upon the earth's rotation. The earth rotates from west to east once every 24 hours. As it rotates, the sun seems to move from east to west.

Because of this, places in the east see the sun before places in the west.

- It is later in the day in places that have already seen the sunrise.

- It is earlier in places that are waiting to see the sun.

New York, for example, is east of California. The sun rises in New York three hours before it rises in California. California must still wait three hours for the sun to rise. Therefore, it is three hours earlier in California than it is New York.

How do we know how many hours difference there are between places?

The earth is divided into 24 standard **time zones**. They are imaginary lines that run north and south. The starting line is called the **prime meridian** [muh-RID-ee-un]. Distance between zones is measured in degrees east or west of the prime meridian.

There is one hour difference between each time zone. For each zone to the east, you add one hour. For each zone to the west, you subtract one hour.

Here's an example. If it is 10 A.M. where you live, then the time in the zone just to the east is 11 A.M. The time zone just to the west is 9 A.M.

Study Figure A. Then answer the questions or fill in the blanks. A through F stand for different places.

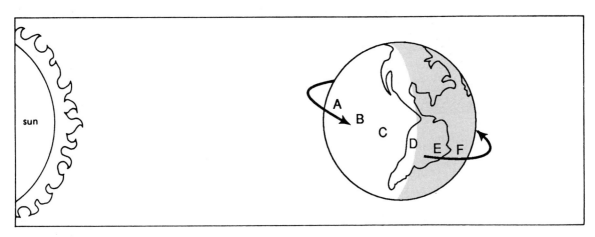

Figure A

1. List the places that are having day: ____A, B, and C____

2. Which of these places had day first? ____C____

3. Which of these places had day last? ____A____

4. In which direction does the earth rotate? ____west to east____
   west to east, east to west

5. As you go to the west, the time becomes ____earlier____ .
   earlier, later

6. As you go to the east, time becomes ____later____ .
   earlier, later

7. B is ____west____ of C. The time at B is ____earlier____ than the time at C.
   east, west   earlier, later

8. B is ____east____ of A. The time at B is ____later____ than the time at A.
   east, west   earlier, later

9. List the places that are having night: ____D E F____

10. Which of these places had night first? ____F____

11. Which of these places had night last? ____D____

12. E is ____east____ of D. The time in E is ____later____ than the time in D.
    east, west   earlier, later

13. E is ____west____ of F. The time at E is ____earlier____ than the time at F.
    east, west   earlier, later

14. Of all the places in the diagram, where is it the earliest? ____A____

15. Of all the places in the diagram, where it it the latest? ____F____

Figure B shows the meridians. Study Figure B. Then answer the questions or fill in the blanks.

1. The direction that meridians travel

   is _____<u>north and south</u>_____ .
   north and south, parallel with the equator

2. The prime meridian passes through

   what city in England? _____

   _____<u>Greenwich</u>_____

3. Distance between meridians is mea–
   sured in degrees (°). How many
   degrees are there between merid–

   ians? _____<u>15°</u>_____

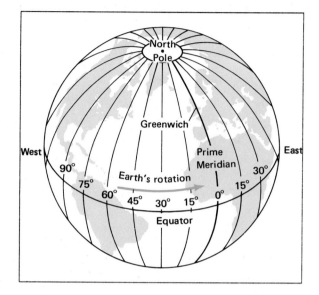

Figure B

The meridians in Figure B are straight lines. The angle between meridians are all the same. But the time zones do not look this way.

Most time zones are not straight lines. They zigzag in order to keep certain related places within the same time zone.

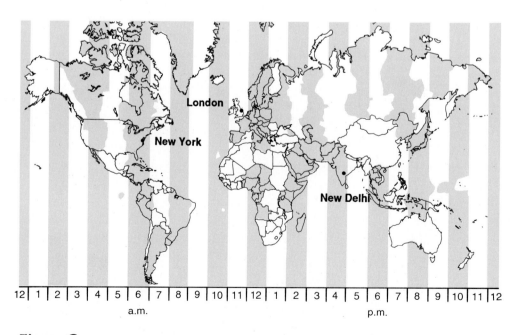

Figure C

4. New York is —————— east —————— of the prime meridian.
   east, west

5. How many hours difference is there between London and New York? ———— 5 ————

6. The time in London is ———— later ———— than the time in New York.
   earlier, later

7. When it is 2 P.M. in New York, what time is it in London?———— 7 P.M. ————

8. When it is 6 A.M. in London, what time is it in New York?———— 1 A.M. ————

9. When it is 1 P.M. in London, what time is it in New Delhi?———— 6 P.M. ————

10. When it is 12 noon in New Delhi, what time is it in London? ———— 7 A.M. ————

NORTH AMERICA'S TIME ZONES

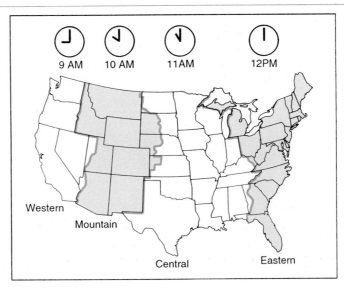

Figure D

Figure D shows the United States. It is divided into four time zones. Study the figure. Answer the questions.

1. Name the time zones in North America.

   Eastern time   Central time

   Mountain time   Pacific time

2. When it is 2 P.M. in the Eastern zone, it is ———— 12 P.M. ———— in the Mountain zone.
   12 P.M., 1 P.M., 4 P.M.

3. When it is 4 A.M. in the Pacific zone, it is ———— 5 A.M. ———— in the Mountain zone.
   3 A.M., 4 A.M., 6 A.M.

4. When it is midnight in the Central zone, it is ———— 10 P.M. ———— in the Pacific zone.
   12 A.M., 1 A.M., 2 A.M.

5. When it is midnight in the Central zone, it is ———— 1 A.M. ———— in the Eastern zone.
   11 P.M., 12 A.M., 2 A.M.

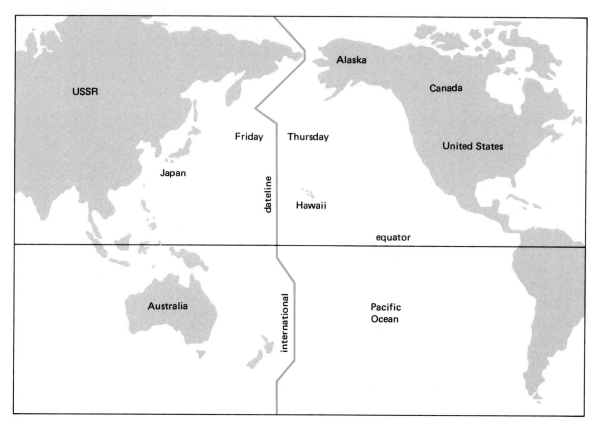

Figure E

Imagine that you are traveling westward. You set your watch back one hour for each meridian you pass. If you travel completely around the world, you will change your watch 24 times. This means your watch would be set one day ahead of every else's watches.

To correct this problem, people agreed that when they crossed a certain meridian, they would change the time on their watches by one day, just like they change their watches by one hour when they enter a new time zone. They called this imaginary line the **international date line.** The international date line is set at the 180° meridian, halfway around the world from the prime meridian.

When you cross the international date line from <u>east to west</u> you <u>add</u> one day. Sunday, for example, becomes Monday.

When you cross the international date line from <u>west to east</u>, you <u>subtract</u> one day. Sunday becomes Saturday.

Now answer these questions:

1. When it is Tuesday in the United States, what day it is in Japan?___Wednesday___

2. When it is Wednesday in Australia, what day is it in Alaska? ____Tuesday____

3. When it is Friday in Hawaii, what day is it in Canada? _____Friday_____

COMPLETING SENTENCES

Choose the correct word or term for each statement. Write your choice in the spaces provided.

1. Time depends upon the earth's _____rotation_____ .
   revolution, rotation

2. The sun seems to move across the sky from _____east to west_____ .
   west to east, east to west

3. Places in the west see the sun _____after_____ places in the east.
   before, after

4. The time in the west is _____earlier_____ than the time in the east.
   earlier, later

5. The time in the east is _____later_____ than the time in the west.
   earlier, later

6. The earth is divided into _____24_____ time zones.
   12, 24, 60

7. Time zones run _____vertically_____ .
   vertically, horizontally

8. The starting time line is called the _____prime meridian_____ .
   prime meridian, international date line

9. The time difference between time zones is one _____hour_____ .
   day, hour, year

10. For each time zone to the east, you _____add_____ one hour.
    add, subtract

11. For each time zone to the west, you _____subtract_____ one hour.
    add, subtract

12. The number of degrees between time zones is _____15_____ .
    90, 15, 180

13. The date changes when you cross the _____international date line_____ .
    prime meridian, international date line

14. It is a day later when you cross the international date line from
    _____east to west_____ .
    west to east, east to west

15. It is a day earlier when you cross the international date line from
    _____west to east_____ .
    west to east, east to west

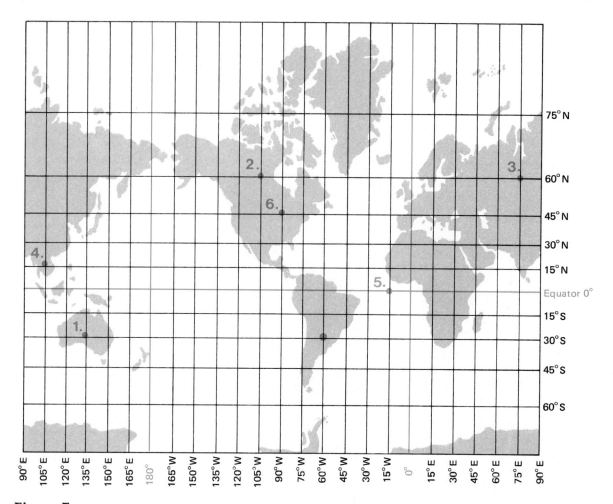

Figure F

The meridians divide the earth into time zones. But they also tell us how far east or west a place is. Location east or west is measured in degrees of longitude.

There are also imaginary lines that run parallel to the equator. These are lines of latitude. They tell us how far north or south of the equator a place is in degrees of latitude.

Look at Figure F. It shows the lines of latitude and longitude. Find the dot that marks the location of 30° south latitude and 60° west longitude. This may be written as 30° S latitude; 60° W longitude.

Now find each of the following locations. Mark each with a dot and its number.

   1. 30° S latitude; 245° E longitude   **2.** 60° N latitude; 105° W longitude

   3. 60° N latitude; 75° E longitude   **4.** 15° N latitude; 105° E longitude

   5. 0° S latitude; 15° W longitude   **6.** 45° N latitude; 90° W longitude

EARTH'S MOTIONS

How does the earth orbit the sun?

13

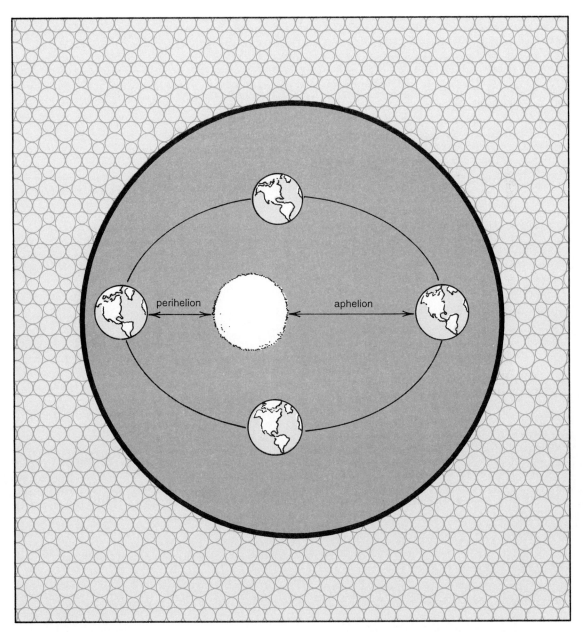

aphelion [af-FEEL-yun]:   point in the earth's orbit where the earth and sun are the farthest apart
ellipse [uh-LIPS]:   oval-shaped
gravity [GRAV-uh-tee]:   force of attraction that exists between all objects in the universe
perihelion [per-uh-HEEL-yun]:   point in the earth's orbit where the earth and sun are the closest

LESSON 13 | How does the earth orbit the sun?

Look at Figure A on the facing page. By now, you know it well. It shows the earth's orbit around the sun.

Notice that the earth's orbit is not in the shape of a circle. The earth's orbit is slightly oval-shaped. This shape is called an **ellipse** [uh-LIPS].

What is the difference between a circle an an ellipse?

In a circle, the distance from the center to any point along the edge is the same.

In an ellipse, the distance from the center to the edge changes as you move along the edge.

An ellipse has a long axis and a short axis. They cross at right angles at the center of the ellipse.

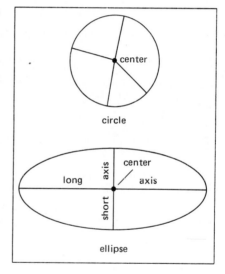

The earth's orbit is an ellipse. And the sun is not exactly in the center of the ellipse. It is slightly off center. For these reasons, the earth is not the same distance from the sun at all times.

About January 2, the earth is closest to the sun. It is about 147 million kilometers away. The point in the orbit that is closest to the sun is called the **perihelion** [per-uh-HEEL-yun].

About July 3, the earth is farthest from the sun. It is about 152 million kilometers away. The point in the orbit that is farthest from the sun is called the **aphelion** [af-FEEL-yun].

All the planets—not just the earth—orbit the sun in elliptical paths.

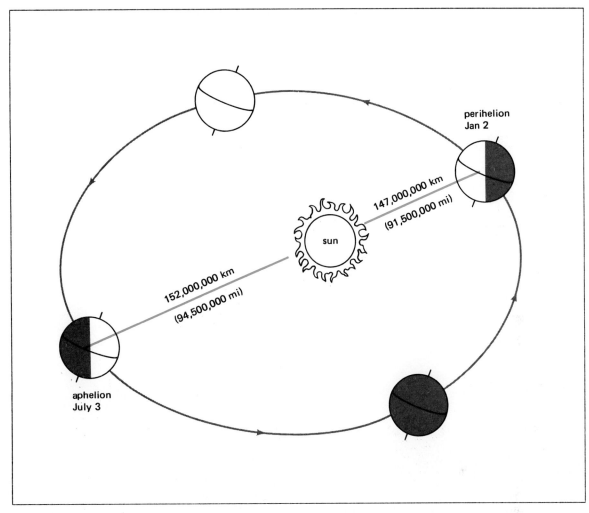

Figure A

1. What is the shape of the earth's orbit?_____ellipse_____

2. Is the sun in the center of the orbit? _____no_____

3. Is the earth the same distance from the sun along the entire orbit?_____no_____

4. How far is the earth from the sun about January 2? _____147,00,000 km_____

5. This is the earth's _____closest_____ distance from the sun.
   closest, farthest

6. What do we call this point of the earth's orbit? _____perihelion_____

7. How far is the earth from the sun about July 3? _____152,000,000 km_____

8. This is the earth's _____farthest_____ distance from the sun.
   closest, farthest

9. What do we call this point of the earth's orbit? _____aphelion_____

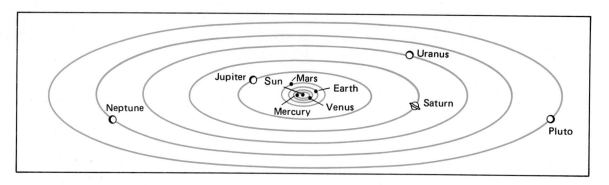

Figure B

A planet moves at different speeds at different points of its orbit. The speed depends upon how close or far away from the sun the planet is.

1. How many planets orbit the sun? _____ 9 _____

2. List the planets in order starting with the planet closest to the sun.

    (1) ___Mercury___   (2) ___Venus___   (3) ___Earth___

    (4) ___Mars___   (5) ___Jupiter___   (6) ___Saturn___

    (7) ___Uranus___   (8) ___Neptune___   (9) ___Pluto___

3. What shape is the orbit of every planet? ___ellipse___

Scientists have found that:

-   The <u>closer</u> a planet is to the sun, the <u>faster</u> it moves.
-   The <u>farther</u> a planet is from the sun, the <u>slower</u> it moves.

The speed of a planet's orbit is called its orbital velocity [OR-buh-tul vuh-LOS-uh-tee]

4. a) Which planet has the slowest orbital velocity? ___Pluto___

    b) Why? ___It is the planet farthest from the sun.___

5. a) Which planet has the fastest orbital velocity? ___Mercury___

    b) Why? ___It is the planet closest from the sun.___

A planet moves at different speeds at different points of its orbit. The speed depends upon how close or far away from the sun the planet is.

6. Look back at Figure A.

    a) On which date does the earth move the fastest? ___January 2___

    b) Why? ___It is closest to the sun on that day.___

7. a) On which date does the earth move the slowest? ___July 3___

    b) Why? ___It is farthest from the sun on that day.___

You throw a ball into the air. It moves upward for a short time. Then it starts falling back to the ground. Why does it fall back? Why doesn't it keep moving upward? A force called gravity pulls it back toward the earth. **Gravity** is a pulling force. It is the force that attracts objects toward one another.

Gravity pulls the earth and anything on the earth towards one another. As you stand on the earth, you are pulled downward, toward the center of the earth.

Every object in the universe pulls on every other object in the universe, from the tiniest atom to the largest star. However, all objects do not have the same gravitational pull. The strength of a gravitational pull depends upon two things. They are the:

AMOUNT OF MATTER in the objects pulling each other. The more matter there is, the stronger the pull. The pull of an atom is tiny. The pull of a star is huge.

DISTANCE between the objects. The closer two objects are to each other, the more they pull on each other. The pull of Earth on you is very large since you are so close to Earth. The pull of Jupiter on you is smaller since Jupiter is so far away.

Gravity holds the planets around the sun and moons around the planets. If there were no gravity the planets would just fly off into space away from the sun.

FILL IN THE BLANK

Complete each statement using a term or terms from the list below. Write your answers in the spaces provided.

matter   moon   downward
sun   gravity   distance between
pulling

1. The force that pulls objects towards one another is called _____gravity_____ .

2. Gravity is a _____pulling_____ force.

3. Gravity pulls things on the earth _____downward_____ .

4. Gravity depends upon two things: the amount of _____matter_____ objects have, and the _____distance between_____ the objects.

5. Gravity keeps the _____moon_____ moving around the Earth. It also keeps the planets moving around the _____sun_____ .

TRUE OR FALSE

In the space provided, write "true" if the sentence is true. Write "false" if the sentence is false.

False 1. The planets move in circular orbits around the sun.

False 2. The sun is in the very center of the earth's orbit.

False 3. The earth is at the same distance from the sun at all times.

True 4. The earth's orbital velocity changes as it moves around the sun.

False 5. Aphelion is the closest point of an orbit.

True 6. Perihelion is the closest point of an orbit.

True 7. The earth is at aphelion in July.

False 8. The earth is closest to the sun in July.

True 9. The closer a planet is to the sun, the faster it moves.

False 10. The orbital velocity of Pluto is faster than the orbital velocity of Earth.

REACHING OUT

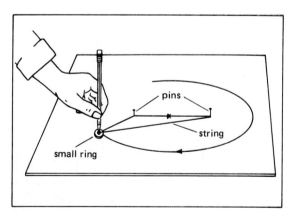

Figure C

You can make an ellipse easily. Figure C shows how to do it.

Make a few ellipses at home.

Try using different string lengths and different pin positions.

What causes the change of seasons?

14

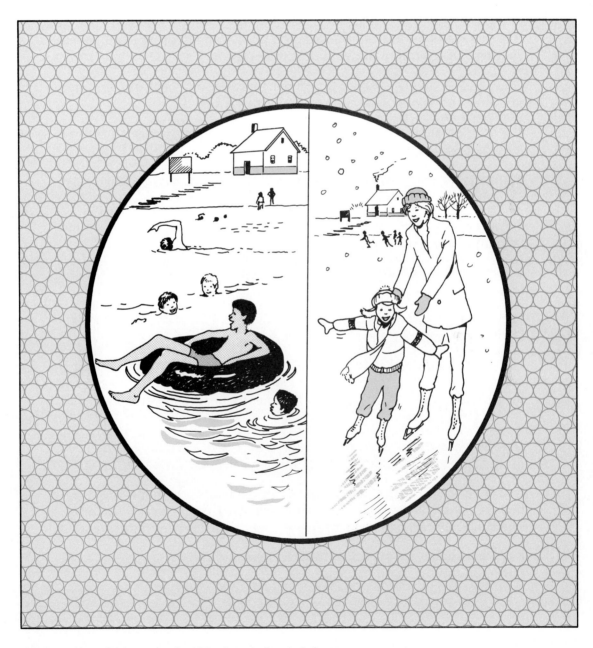

direct rays: light rays that hit the earth straight on
indirect rays: light rays that do not hit the earth straight on

LESSON 14 | What causes the change of seasons?

Are you ready for a vacation? Will you go swimming or will you go ice-skating? Of course, it all depends on the season.

Most people live in places that have four seasons—spring, summer, autumn, and winter.

The four seasons are marked by differences in temperature and in the lengths of day and night.

Summer, for example, is much warmer than winter. And summer days are longer than winter days.

What causes seasons? Seasons are caused by the earth's revolution around the sun and the unchanging tilt of the earth's axis.

You have already learned how the earth's axis causes differences in the lengths of day and night. The axis also causes differences in temperature.

Part of the year, the axis leans towards the sun. Part of the year, the axis leans away from the sun.

For example, June 21 is the first day of summer in the Northern Hemisphere. On that day, the Northern Hemisphere leans toward the sun the most. The sun's rays strike head-on or nearly head-on over a large part of this hemisphere.

Direct rays are rays that are head on. Direct rays are strong rays. They do not spread over a large area. Direct rays heat up the earth the most.

December 21 is the first day of winter in the Northern Hemisphere. On that day, the Northern Hemisphere leans away from the sun the most. The sun's rays do not strike head-on. They spread over a large area.

Rays that spread out are called **indirect rays**. Indirect rays are weak rays. They heat up the earth the least.

Figure A shows direct rays and indirect rays. Study it. Then answer the questions or fill in the blanks.

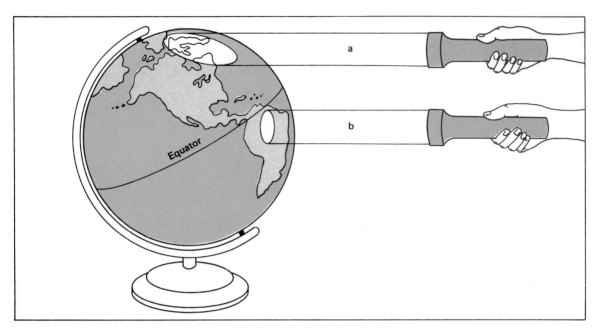

Figure A

1. Which rays are direct? _____ b _____
   a, b

2. Which rays are indirect? _____ a _____
   a, b

Answer "direct" or "indirect".

3. Which rays spread out? _____ indirect _____

4. Which rays do not spread out? _____ direct _____

5. Which rays are stronger? _____ direct _____

6. Which rays are weaker? _____ indirect _____

7. Which rays heat a place more? _____ direct _____

8. Which rays heat a place less? _____ indirect _____

9. Winter rays are _____ indirect _____ rays.

10. Summer rays are _____ direct _____ rays.

11. Which of the rays of Figure A can stand for winter rays? _____ a _____
    a, b

12. Which of the rays on Figure A can stand for summer rays? _____ b _____
    a, b

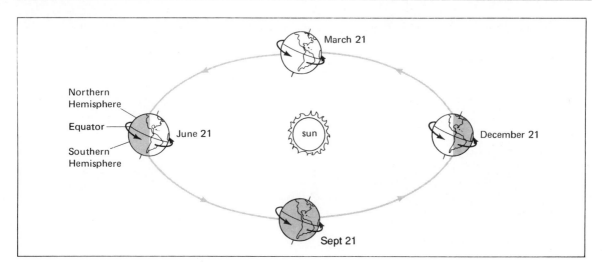

Figure B

TAKE A TRIP. Follow the earth for one revolution around the sun. Study Figure B. Then fill in the blanks.

1. The earth revolves around the sun in a ___counterclockwise___ direction.
   clockwise, counterclockwise

2. As the earth revolves around the sun, the earth's axis ___does not___ change.
   does, does not

3. **On June 21, the Northern Hemisphere . . .**

   a) faces ___toward___ the sun.
      toward, away from

   b) has mainly ___warm___ weather.
      cold, warm

   c) has ___more___ hours of daylight than the Southern Hemisphere.
      more, fewer

   d) receives ___direct___ rays. These are ___strong___ rays.
      direct, slanting   strong, weak

   e) has the first day of ___summer___ .
      summer, fall, winter, spring

4. **Between June 21 and September 20, . . .**

   a) the Northern Hemisphere still leans toward the sun, but every day the lean

   becomes ___less___ .
   greater, less

   b) the rays become ___less___ direct and spread out ___more___ .
      more, less   more, less

   c) the days become___shorter___ and the nights become___longer___ .
      longer, shorter   longer, shorter

5. On September 21 . . .

a) the earth's axis is tilted __neither toward or away from__ the sun.
   toward, away from, neither toward nor away from

b) the sun's rays are __neither direct or indirect__ .
   direct, indirect, neither direct nor indirect

c) __fall__ starts in the Northern Hemisphere.
   summer, fall, winter, spring

d) every place on Earth has __12__ hours of day and

   __12__ hours of night.

6. Between September 21 and December 20 . . .

a) the Northern Hemisphere starts to lean __away from__ the sun.
   toward, away from

b) the sun's rays become more __indirect__ . These rays are
   direct, indirect

   __weaker__ .
   stronger, weaker

c) days become __shorter__ and nights become __longer__ .
   longer, shorter   longer, shorter

7. On December 21 the Northern Hemisphere . . .

a) faces __away from__ the sun.
   toward, away from

b) has mainly __cold__ weather.
   cold, warm

c) has __fewer__ hours of daylight than the Southern Hemisphere.
   more, fewer

d) receives __indirect__ rays. These are __weak__ rays.
   direct, indirect   strong, weak

e) has the first day of __winter__ .
   summer, fall, winter, spring

8. Between December 21 and March 20 . . .

a) the Northern Hemisphere leans away from the sun, but every day the lean

   becomes __less__ .
   more, less

b) the rays become __less__ slanting.
   more, less

c) the days become __longer__ and the nights become __shorter__ .
   longer, shorter   longer, shorter

81

9. **On March 21 . . .**

   a) the earth's axis is tilted ___neither toward nor away from___ the sun.

   toward, away from, neither toward nor away from

   b) the sun's rays are ___neither direct nor indirect___ .

   direct, indirect, neither direct nor indirect

   c) ___spring___ starts in the Northern Hemisphere.

   summer, fall, winter, spring

10. **Between March 21 and June 21 . . .**

   a) the Northern Hemisphere starts to lean ___toward___ the sun.

   toward, away from

   b) the rays become more and more ___direct___ .

   direct, indirect

   c) the rays become ___stronger___ .

   stronger, weaker

   d) the days become ___longer___ and the nights become ___shorter___ .

   longer, shorter   longer, shorter

11. In the Northern Hemisphere, the number of daylight hours is greatest on

   ___June 21___ ; this is the first day of ___summer___ .

   March 21, June 21, September 23, December 20   summer, fall, winter, spring

CONGRATULATIONS! YOUR TRIP AROUND THE SUN IS NOW COMPLETE!

12. How long did your trip take? ___one year___

REACHING OUT

Record-breaking temperatures rarely happen on the first day of summer. It is usually the later months of summer that have the hottest weather. Why?

Accept all logical responses. Likely responses include that it takes time for the sun's

rays to slowly warm the Earth up. Therefore there is a time delay between the longest

day of the year and the warmest day of the year.

What is known about the earth's moon?

15

craters [KRAY-turz]:   round holes on the moon's surface
lunar: related to the moon
maria [MAHR-ee-uh]:   broad, flat plains on the moon
meteorite [MEE-tee-or-ite]:   piece of rock or metal that hits the earth's surface

LESSON 15 | What is known about the earth's moon?

"That's one small step for a man — one giant leap for mankind."

The date was July 20, 1969. And with those historic words, astronaut Neil Armstrong became the first person to set foot on the moon. For two hours, he and fellow astronaut, Edwin Aldrin, walked on its surface. They took pictures, collected rocks, and performed experiments.

Altogether, twelve astronauts (all American), have explored the moon's surface. Several scientific instruments were left behind. They sent back valuable moon data.

To the unaided eye, the moon's surface, also called the **lunar** surface, seems little more then patches of light and dark areas. However, with a telescope, we can see a variety of features. Three of the most noticeable features are <u>maria</u>, <u>craters</u>, and <u>mountains</u>.

MARIA Galileo, the famous astronomer, studied the moon through his telescope. He thought the basins were filled with water — and named them **maria** [MAHR-ee-uh]. *Maria* is the Latin word for seas.

Lunar "seas" are not seas at all. They contain no water. In fact, there is no water <u>or</u> air on the moon . . . None at all! Lunar "seas" are really broad and generally smooth <u>plains</u>. They look dark because their dark rock reflects less light than surrounding high areas. The lunar maria were formed from hardened lava flows.

Now we know that these "seas" are dry. But the name remains. Actually, both terms are used — <u>seas</u> and <u>maria</u>.

CRATERS Craters [KRAY-turz] are impressions on the moon's surface. They are generally round with rugged rims.

Craters are formed when **meteorites** [MEE-tee-or-ites] impact upon the moon's surface. The entire moon's surface — even the maria are pocked with craters. In fact, some craters have even smaller craters.

Craters vary in size — from microscopic size to ones several hundred feet across. More than 30,000 craters have been mapped. If we included the very tiny ones, there would be too many to count.

MOUNTAINS Lunar mountains, are, indeed, MOUNTAINS. Some tower 18,000 feet — and more. The tallest lunar mountain is 1,930 meters (26,000 feet) high. That's nearly 5 miles.

Figure A

"That's one small step for a man, one giant leap for mankind." Neil Armstrong said these words as he became the first person to set foot on the moon. Figure A shows a photo that Armstrong took of his fellow astronaut, Edwin Aldrin.

If you look closely at Aldrin's visor, you can see the reflection of Neil Armstrong taking the picture.

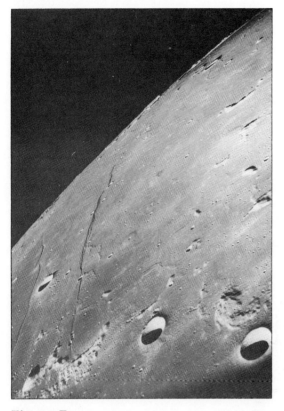

Figure B

The moon's surface is constantly bombarded by meteorites. When meteorites hit the moon, impact craters are formed. In some places on the moon, there are so many craters that new craters simply cover up old craters. When lava formed the lunar maria, it covered up all the craters that had previously been there. As a result, the maria only have craters from meteorites which struck the moon after the lava hardened. Therefore, there are fewer craters in the maria.

Meteorites constantly enter the earth's atmosphere as well. Yet almost all burn up in the atmosphere long before they could crash onto the surface.

Figure C

Meteorites can be any size. Some are very very small. Even tiny micrometeorites can form craters. They impact at speeds of up to 40 kilometers (64 miles) per second surface. This never ending "sandblasting" pits the moon's surface.

Figure D

Impacts from meteorites break up some of the moon's rock into a fine dust. The moon's surface is covered with this fine grey-brown dust.

TRUE OR FALSE

In the space provided, write "true" if the sentence is true. Write "false" if the sentence is false.

False   **1.** A telescope makes things larger.

False   **2.** Galileo is a modern-day scientist.

False   **3.** Lunar seas contain water.

False   **4.** The Moon can support life.

True   **5.** Craters on the Moon were formed by meteorite impacts.

True   **6.** All lunar seas have craters.

False   **7.** Lunar seas show up as light patches.

True   **8.** Lunar craters can be found in many sizes.

FILL IN THE BLANK

Complete each statement using a term or terms from the list below. Write your answers in the spaces provided.

lava	maria	craters
round	moon	sizes
smooth	micrometeorites	flat
meteorites		

1. The earth's only natural satellite is the ___moon___ .

2. Lunar maria are dry areas that are generally ___flat___ and ___smooth___ .

3. Another name for lunar "seas" is ___maria___ .

4. Depressions that dot the lunar surface are called ___craters___ .

5. Lunar "seas" were formed from hardened ___lava___ .

6. Highly visible lunar craters were caused by impacting ___meteorites___ .

7. Craters are generally ___round___ and are found in a great range of ___sizes___ .

8. The tiniest craters are caused by the impact of ___micrometeorites___ .

MATCHING

Match each term in Column A with its description in Column B. Write the correct letter in the space provided.

	Column A		Column B
b	1. telescope	a)	molten volcanic material
d	2. maria	b)	useful scientific tool
e	3. crater	c)	rock material from space
a	4. lava	d)	lunar seas
c	5. meteorite	e)	created by meteorite impacts

REACHING OUT

Figure E *A photo of the moon taken by Apollo 17 astronauts.*

We now know for certain. The moon has no air and no water. Do you think there is life on the moon? Why? Living things need air and water to survive. Since there is no air or water on the moon, there cannot be any life there.

Why can we see only one side of the moon?

16

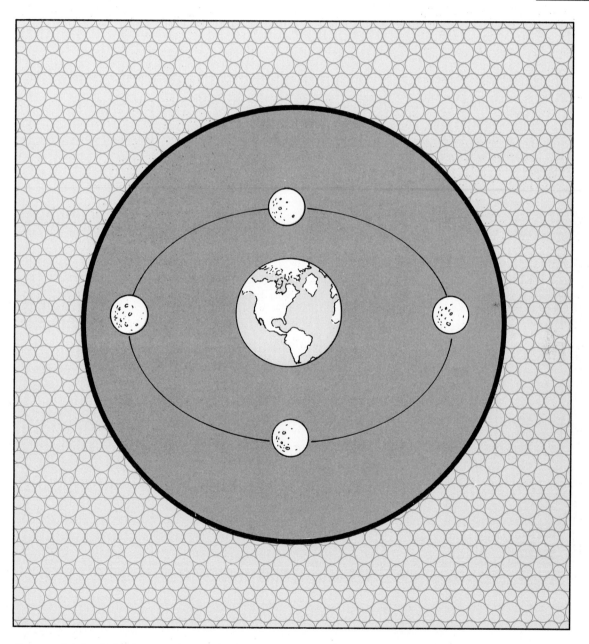

apogee [AP-uh-jee]:   point at which the moon is farthest from the earth
perigee [PER-uh-jee]:   point at which the moon is closest to the earth

LESSON 16 | Why can we see only one side of the moon?

On August 10, 1956, an Atlas Agena rocket blasted off from Kennedy Space Flight Center. It carried an unmanned satellite—Lunar Orbiter 1. Four days later, Orbiter 1 was circling the moon. This satellite sent back many pictures. Some showed the back half of the moon.

From the earth, we can see only one side of the moon. The other side of the moon always faces away from us.

Why does only one side of the moon face us? The explanation is really simple.

Like the earth, the moon rotates. That is, it turns around its own axis. While the moon is rotating, it is also revolving. It is moving around the earth.

• One moon rotation takes 27 1/3 days.

• One moon revolution takes the same time—27 1/3 days.

The periods of rotation and revolution are the same. The moon turns around its center once for each time it moves around the earth.

Because of this, only one side of the moon faces us. The opposite side always is hidden from the earth.

Have you ever seen a top spinning? How about a gymnast doing a flip? Both of these motions involve rotation. Rotation is the spinning of an object around its axis. The moon also rotates around its axis.

Figure A *Rotation*

Imagine you are the dancer in Figure A. During one rotation, you will face in every direction of the circle. At the end of one rotation, you will face the same direction as when you started.

1. List the points you expect to see as you turn. _____A, B, C, D_____

2. Will you see the places between these points? _____yes_____

3. After one quarter turn, which point do you see?_____D_____

4. After two one-quarter turns, which point do you see? _____A_____

5. Two one-quarter turns equals which fraction of one turn?_____1/2_____
   1/4, 1/2, 3/4

6. Look at your starting position. At one half turn, the direction you face is

   _____just opposite_____ .
   the same, just opposite

7. At three one-quarter turns, which point do you see? _____B_____

8. Three one-quarter turns equals which fraction of one turn? _____3/4_____
   1/4, 1/2, 3/4

9. When you make one more quarter turn, which point do you see again?_____C_____

10. a) Did you rotate? _____yes_____

    b) Did you revolve? _____no_____

    c) How do you know? ___I know that I rotated because I faced every direction. I___
    ___know that I did not revolve because I did not go around anything.___

Revolution is the movement of an object all the way around another object.

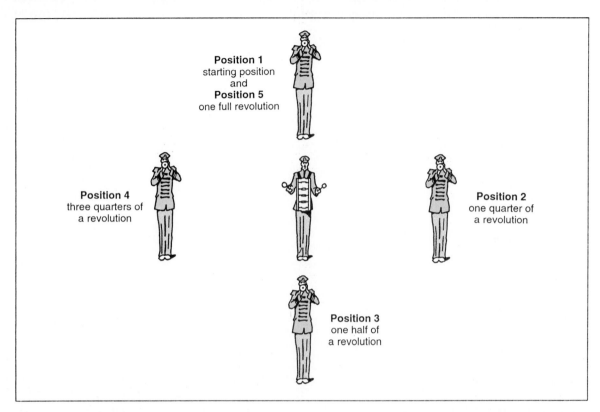

Figure B *Revolution*

Figure B shows a trumpet player revolving around a drum player. The trumpet player is playing his trumpet while he is revolving. He always faces towards the audience. He faces forward. Imagine you are the trumpet player in Figure B. Answer the following questions.

1. After one quarter revolution, what will you see? _____the audience_____

2. After one half of a revolution, what will you see? _____the audience_____

3. After three quarters of a revolution, what will you see? _____the audience_____

4. After one full revolution, what will you see? _____the audience_____

5. Did you always face the same direction? _____yes_____

6. Did you rotate? _____no_____

7. Did you travel all the way around the drummer? _____yes_____

8. Did you revolve? _____yes_____

9. When an object revolves, can it also rotate? _____yes_____

10. When an object revolves, must it also rotate? _____no_____

Imagine that you are walking (revolving) around a chair. The diagram below shows what you look like.

Study the diagram. Then answer the questions.

Figure C *Rotation and Revolution together*

1. How many revolutions have you made? _____one_____

2. At half way through the revolution, you were facing ___the opposite___

    _{the opposite, the same}

    direction as when you started.

3. At one revolution, you were facing ___the same___ direction as when you started.

    _{the opposite, the same}

4. What were you doing while you were revolving? ___rotating___

5. How many times? ___once___

6. As you were revolving and rotating, how many sides of your body faced the chair?

    ___one___

    _{one, two, three, all}

7. When an object rotates once for each time it revolves around an object

    ___only one side faces the object___ .

    _{only one side faces the object, all sides face the object}

93

The moon revolves around the earth in an elliptical orbit at a speed of 3500 kilometers per hour. It takes 27 1/3 days to make one complete revolution.

The point in the orbit where the moon is farthest from the earth is called **apogee** [AP-uh-jee]. The distance from the moon to the earth during apogee is 409,000 kilometers. The point in the orbit where the moon is closest to the earth is called **perigee** [PER-uh-gee]. The distance from the moon to the earth during perigee is 365,000 kilometers.

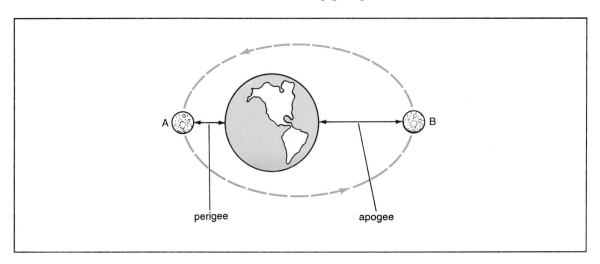

Figure D

Use Figure D to answer the following questions.

1. When the moon is closest to the earth, it is at _____perigee_____ .

2. When the moon is farthest fron the earth, it is at_____apogee_____ .

3. The moon takes _____27 1/3_____ days to make one complete revolution around the earth.

4. The moon takes _____27 1/3_____ days to make one complete rotation on its axis.

5. Why does the same side of the moon always face the earth? _____The moon_____ revolves at the same speed as it rotates, therefore we only see one side of the moon.

Use the diagram to complete the following.

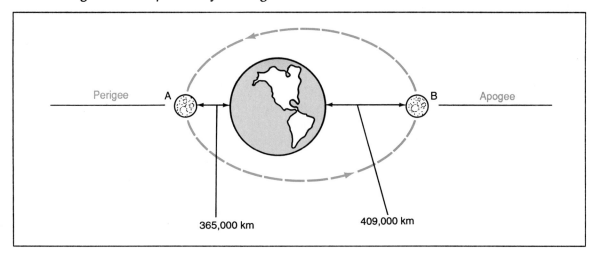

Figure E   *The elliptical orbit of the moon.*

1. The diagram shows the distance of the moon from the earth at apogee and at perigee. Label each of these positions on the diagram in the space provided.

2. What is the distance of the moon from the earth at apogee? ___409,000 km___

3. What is the distance of the moon from the earth at perigee? ___365,000 km___

4. How much closer to the earth is the moon at perigee than at apogee?

   ___44,000 km___

MATCHING

Match each term in Column A with its description in Column B. Write the correct letter in the space provided.

	Column A		Column B
__d__	1. apogee	a)	when the earth is closest to the moon
__a__	2. perigee	b)	spinning of an object around its axis
__e__	3. revolution	c)	moon related
__b__	4. rotation	d)	when the earth is farthest from the moon
__c__	5. lunar	e)	movement of an object around another

The earth's rotation brings the moon into view every day. Like the sun, the moon appears to rise in the east and set in the west. The moon rises and sets a little later each day. For example, suppose you saw the moon rise at 8:00 PM on Monday. On Tuesday, you would see the moon rise at 8:50 PM.

As the moon revolves around the earth, the earth must rotate through more than one complete rotation to "catch up" with the moon. The earth must rotate 24 hours and 50 minutes to bring the moon back into the same position that you have seen it the night before. As a result, the moon rises 50 minutes later each day.

1. From the earth, the moon appears to rise in the _____east_____ .

2. From the earth, the moon appears to set in the _____west_____.

3. The moon rises and sets _____50 minutes_____ later each day.

4. If the moon rose at 5:00 PM on Friday, what time would it rise on Saturday?

   _____5:50 PM_____ .

5. If the moon set at 5:30 AM on Wednesday, what time would it set on Thursday?

   _____6:20 AM_____

REACHING OUT

The word "month" comes from a variation of the Greek word meaning "moon." Use a dictionary or other reference source and find out how the word "month" got its name. Write this information in the space provided.

Student responses should indicate that in ancient times, the passage of time was

measured using the moon. The time between one full moon and the next full moon

is called a lunar month.

_____

_____

What are the phases of the moon?

17

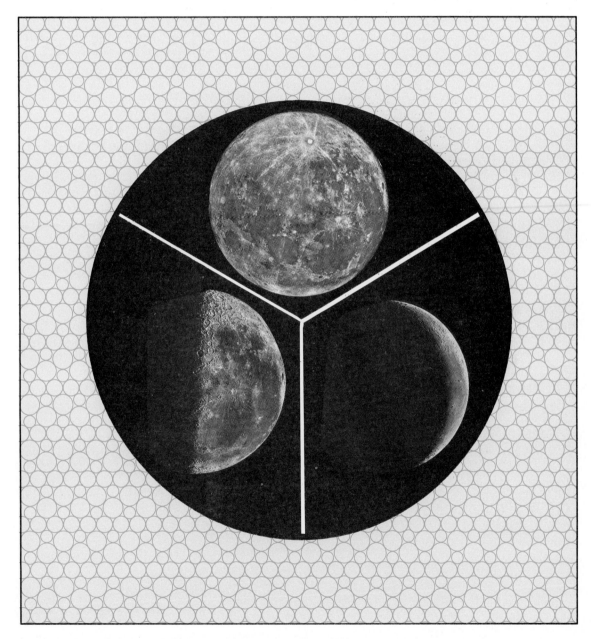

phases [FAYZ-uz]:   changing shapes of the moon
waning [WAYN-ning]:   after the full moon; as the visible part of the moon decreases
waxing: after a new moon; as the visible part of the moon increases

LESSON 17 | What are the phases of the moon?

The moon does not give off its own light like the sun does. It shines by reflected light. The sun shines on the moon. The moon then reflects this light from the sun to our eyes.

You can see the moon shining brightly on almost any clear night. But from night to night, the moon seems to change its shape. The different shapes the moon seems to have are called **phases** [FAYZ-uz]. Figure A shows the phases.

If you look at the moon every night, you will notice that the phases always follow one another in the same order. First the moon may look like a large white disk. Then it seems to shrink and disappear only to start "growing" again.

Why does the moon seem to change shape? The moon revolves, or orbits, around the earth. One orbit takes about 27 1/3 days. During this time, about half of the moon is always lit up. But, most of the time we cannot see all this light.

How much moonlight we see depends upon where the moon is in its orbit. At full moon, we see all of the lit side. At new moon, we see none of the lit side. At all other phases, we see part of the lit side.

Figure A shows the moon in orbit. Study it and then answer the questions or fill in the blanks below.

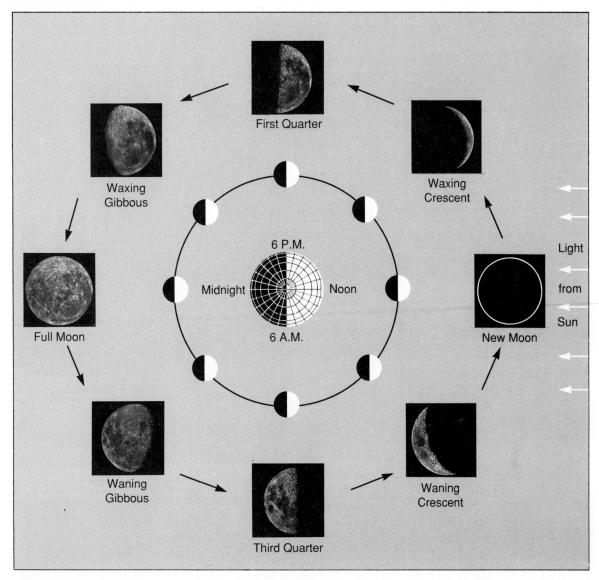

Figure A

The side of the moon facing the sun is always lit up. But we cannot see all of this lit up area every night. The boxes show how the moon looks to us from the earth. Notice how its shape seems to change during the orbit.

1. What do we call the different shapes the moon seems to have? _____ phases _____

2. Where does the moon get its light? _____ the sun _____

3. How much of the moon is always bright? _____ one half _____

4. Can we see all this light every night? _____ no _____

5. At which phase can we see <u>all</u> of the lighted half of the Moon? _____ full moon _____

6. At which phase can we see none of the lighted half of the Moon? __new moon__

7. At which phases can we see one half of the lighted half of the Moon?
   __first quarter__   __third quarter__

8. At which phases can we see less than one half of the lighted part of the Moon?
   __waning crescent__   __waxing crescent__

9. At which phases can we see more than one half, but not all of the lighted half of the Moon. __waning gibbous__   __waxing gibbous__

10. At new moon, the lighted half of the moon faces ___away from___ the earth.
    towards, away from

11. At full moon, the lighted half of the moon faces ___towards___ the earth.
    towards, away from

12. Between new moon and full moon the moon seems to ___grow___ in size.
    grow, shrink

13. Between full moon and new moon, the moon seems to ___shrink___ in size.
    grow, shrink

14. How long does the moon take to orbit the earth? __27 1/3 days__

COMPLETE THE CHART

The figures below show the eight phases of the Moon. Complete the chart below by writing the correct figure letter or letters in the space provided.

Figure B   Figure C   Figure D   Figure E   Figure F   Figure G   Figure H   Figure I

	Phase	Figure
1.	Gibbous moons	C I
2.	New moon	F
3.	Crescent moons	E G
4.	Full moon	B
5.	Quarter moons	D H

FILL IN THE BLANK

Complete each statement using a term or terms from the list below. Write your answers in the spaces provided. Some words may be used more than once.

sun	new crescent	phases
full moon	reflects	orbits
change	moon	one half
old crescent	new moon	

1. Our closest neighbor in space is the _____ moon _____ .

2. The moon gets its light from the _____ Sun _____ . Some light from the

   moon _____ reflects _____ onto Earth.

3. About _____ one half _____ of the moon is always bright.

4. The shape of the moon seems to _____ change _____ .

5. The different shapes that the moon seems to have ar called _____ phases _____ .

6. The different shapes that the moon seems to have depend upon how much of its light

   _____ reflects _____ back to the Earth.

7. The moon changes appearance because it _____ orbits _____ the Earth.

8. At _____ new moon _____ we cannot see the moon.

9. At _____ full moon _____ we see about one whole side of the moon.

10. The phases that show least of the moon are _____ new crescent _____ and

    _____ old crescent _____ .

TRUE OR FALSE

In the space provided, write "true" if the sentence is true. Write "false" if the sentence is false.

_____ False _____ 1. The earth orbits the moon.

_____ False _____ 2. The moon gives off its own light.

_____ True _____ 3. The moon reflects light from the sun.

_____ True _____ 4. About one half of the moon is always lit.

_____ False _____ 5. We can always see the lit half of the moon.

CROSSWORD PUZZLE

Use the clues to complete the crossword puzzle.

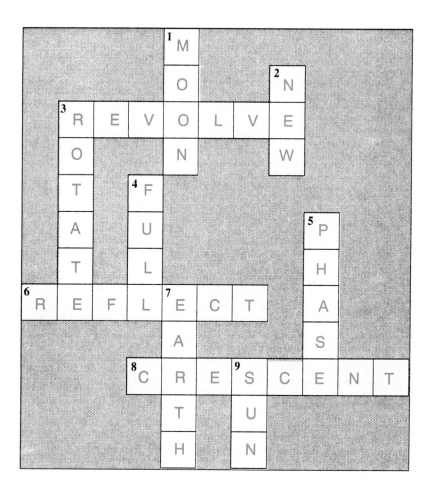

Clues

Across

3. What the moon does around the earth

6. What the moon does to light from the sun

8. Phase of the moon when only a small part can be seen

Down

1. Revolves around the earth

2. Phase of the moon when it cannot be seen

3. Spin

4. Phase of moon when one whole side can be seen

7. Planet you are on

9. Star nearest to earth

What is a solar eclipse? 18

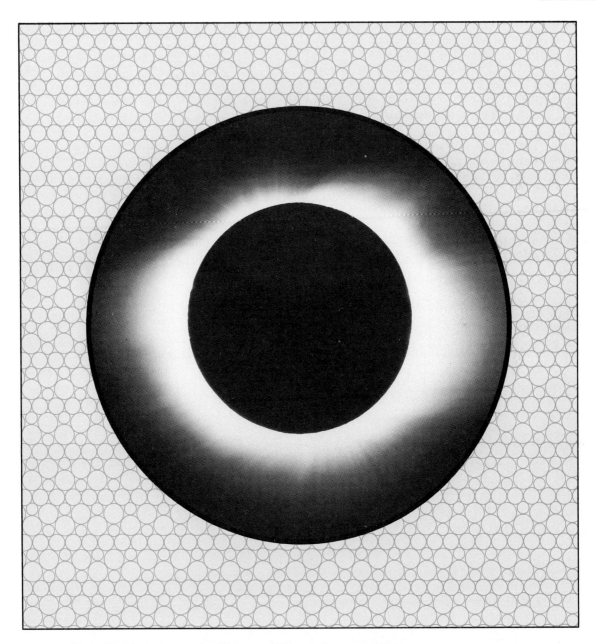

corona [kuh-ROH-nuh]:   outer layer of the sun's atmosphere
solar eclipse [SOH-ler uh-CLIPS]:   passing of the moon between the earth and the sun

LESSON 18 | What is a solar eclipse?

Everyone has seen shadows. You have seen shadows of trees, buildings, and fences. How often have you noticed your own shadow following you? You can see a shadow right now! Just hold your hand close to this page. What do you see on the page?

What is a shadow? A shadow is an area of darkness. It forms when an object gets in the way or blocks light.

Every object that blocks light forms a shadow. The earth and moon are no exceptions. The earth and moon block the sun's light. They cast huge cone-shaped shadows deep into space.

The earth and moon are always moving. Sometimes the earth moves behind the moon. Part of the earth is in the moon's shadow. For the people at this place on earth, the moon blocks out, or eclipses, the sun. The eclipsed area becomes dark. For a short period of time, it looks like it is night time.

A **solar eclipse** [SOH-ler uh-CLIPS] takes place when the sun, moon and Earth are in a straight or almost straight line with the moon between the sun and the Earth.

A solar eclipse does not last long — no longer than a few minutes in any one place.

Since scientists know a lot about the orbits of the Earth and the moon, they can accurately predict:

- <u>when</u> an eclipse will take place
- <u>where</u> it will take place
- <u>how long</u> it will last

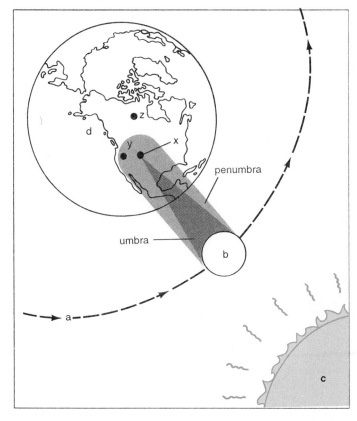

Figure A

Figure A shows a solar eclipse. Study it and answer the questions.

Identify the following by letter.

_____c_____ **1.** sun

_____d_____ **2.** earth

_____b_____ **3.** moon

_____a_____ **4.** moon's orbit

A shadow has a dark middle part, and a lighter outer part.

5. What do we call the darker middle part? _____umbra_____

6. What do we call the lighter outer part? _____penumbra_____

7. Which part of the shadow covers a wider area?

_____penumbra_____

Figure B

Figure B shows a multiple exposure of a solar eclipse.

The top left shows the sun before the moon moves in front of it.

In the following images, the moon covers up more and more of the sun.

The sun then reappears at the bottom right.

105

TOTAL SOLAR ECLIPSES

There are two main kinds of solar eclipses — total solar eclipses, and partial solar eclipses.

Figure C shows the sun during a total solar eclipse. The sun is completely blocked. Only light from its rim or **corona** [kuh-ROH-nuh] can be seen.

Figure C *Total solar eclipse*

Look back at Figure A.

1. Where on earth would you be to see what is shown in Figure C? ___x___

   x, y, z

2. This area is called the

   ___umbra___.

   umbra, penumbra

3. It is an area of

   ___complete darkness___.

   full light, reduced light, complete darkness

PARTIAL SOLAR ECLIPSE

Figure D shows the sun during a partial eclipse. Part of the sun seems "chopped off."

Figure D *Partial solar eclipse*

Look back at Figure A again.

4. Where would you be to experience a partial solar eclipse? ___y___

   x, y, z

5. This area is called the

   ___penumbra___.

   umbra, penumbra

6. It is an area of

   ___reduced light___.

   full light, reduced light, complete darkness

7. Imagine that you are in area "z." Would you see an eclipse? ___no___

8. Why? _The moon is not blocking the_

   sun's light.

Figure E

During an eclipse, the moon moves in its orbit around the earth and the earth rotates. Therefore, the place on the surface of the earth that is in the moon's shadow changes. As the eclipse moves slowly across the earth, different people in different places see it at different times. Figure E shows the path of the total solar eclipse of February 26, 1979. The next such eclipse that can be seen from North America will be in the year 2017.

TRUE OR FALSE

In the space provided, write "true" if the sentence is true. Write "false" if the sentence is false.

__True__   **1.** A solid object can cast a shadow.

__True__   **2.** The earth and moon cast shadows.

__True__   **3.** Light is needed for a shadow to form.

__False__   **4.** During a solar eclipse, we cannot see the moon.

__False__   **5.** During a solar eclipse, the earth is between the sun and the moon.

__False__   **6.** A solar eclipse can be seen from any part of the earth that is having daylight at the time of the eclipse.

__True__   **7.** The place to see a solar eclipse changes.

__False__   **8.** A solar eclipse lasts a long time.

__True__   **9.** Partial solar eclipses can be seen in more places than total solar eclipses.

__False__   **10.** You can always see the sun's corona.

MATCHING

Match each term in Column A with its description in Column B. Write the correct letter in the space provided.

	Column A		Column B
__b__	**1.** umbra	**a)**	sun's halo
__e__	**2.** penumbra	**b)**	darker part of a shadow
__d__	**3.** solar eclipse	**c)**	usually are not in a line
__a__	**4.** corona	**d)**	sun blocked out
__c__	**5.** sun, earth, and moon	**e)**	lighter part of a shadow

FILL IN THE BLANK

Complete each statement using a term or terms from the list below. Write your answers in the spaces provided. Some words may be used more than once.

solar eclipse	sun	total
earth	eclipse	darkness
partial	moves	moon
shadows	blocks	corona

1. A shadow is an area of _____darkness_____ .

2. A shadow forms when an object _____blocks_____ light.

3. The _____earth_____ and _____moon_____ block the sun's light. They

   cast long, cone-shaped _____shadows_____ .

4. Sometimes the shadow of a heavenly body blocks out another heavenly body. This

   is called an _____eclipse_____ .

5. The blocking out of the sun by the moon's shadow is called a_____solar eclipse_____ .

6. A solar eclipse occurs when the _____moon_____ is between the

   _____sun_____ and the _____earth_____ .

7. When the moon blocks out all of the sun, we have a_____total_____ solar

   eclipse.

8. When the moon blocks out a part of the sun, we have a _____partial_____

   solar eclipse.

9. During a total eclipse, we can see only the sun's rim. This is called the

   _____corona_____ .

10. The place where you can see a solar eclipse _____moves_____ across part of the

    earth's surface.

REACHING OUT

A solar eclipse can take place only during one moon phase. Which phase is it? Why?

A new moon occurs when the moon is between the earth and the sun which is where

the moon must be during a solar eclipse.

SCIENCE *EXTRA*

Midnight 1991 — A Most Unusual Moment

Happy New Year! Midnight 1991 was very special. It marked an event that happens only once in a blue moon and the new year arrived one second late. Confused? Do not be. The explanations are interesting — and easy to understand.

You have learned about the moon phases. They range from a full moon to a new moon. The moon is full every 29 days, 12 hours, 44 minutes, and 29 seconds. But every month has 30 or 31 days, except for February, which has 28 days.

We see that each month has more time than it takes to complete one moon cycle. Therefore, in each month, a little bit of an additional phase is left over. These extra bits add up. As a result, sometimes, we have two full moons in one month. When this happens, the second full moon is called a blue moon. Why blue? No one knows.

A month with two full moons does not occur often — just once every two and a half years or so. This is where the term "once in a blue moon" comes from. "Once in a blue moon" means "not very often."

That explains why New Year's Eve marked an event that happens once in a blue moon, but why was it one second late?

Our system of time is based upon the rotation of the earth. It is based upon a constant rotation speed. That is where the problem arises! The earth's rotation speed is not constant.

On average, the earth's rotation is slowing. This deceleration is caused by friction, like the slowing of a spinning top. The tides of the oceans rub against the continents creating this friction. On average, the earth's rotation slows about 1/500 second each day. After 500 days, the earth's rotation has slowed by one second.

We now have ultra-accurate atomic clocks. So that the earth and these clocks are in sync, scientists add a second to the atomic clock. This added second is called a leap second.

The U.S. Naval Observatory in Washington D.C. is our nations timekeeper. There scientists like Brian Luzum and Dr. Dennis D. McCarthy, keep track of the earth's rotation. They decide if and when a leap second should be added. The first leap second was added in 1972. The seventeenth leap second was added on (you guessed it) December 31, 1990 just before midnight. Therefore, the new year arrived one second late.

What is a lunar eclipse? 19

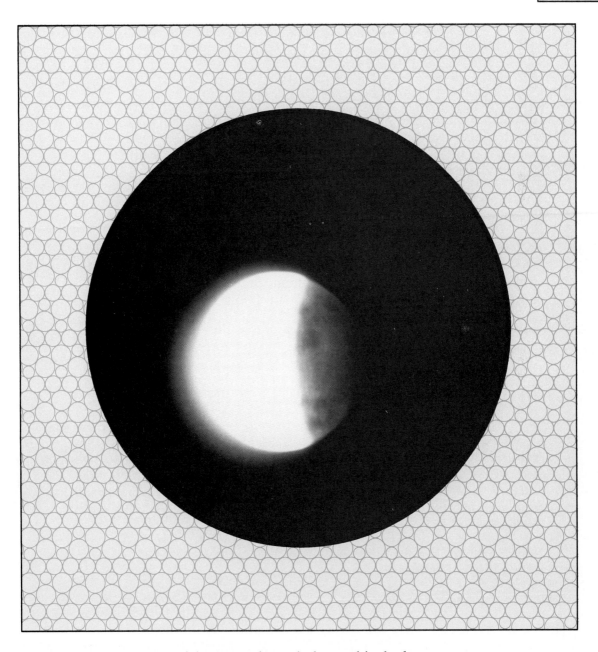

lunar eclipse: passing of the moon through the earth's shadow

LESSON 19 | What is a lunar eclipse?

As you know, the moon does not give off its own light. The moon gets its light from the sun. The light then reflects onto the earth.

The moon revolves around the earth. Most of the time the moon does not move into the earth's shadow. But sometimes it does. Since the earth is much bigger than the moon, the earth has a much bigger shadow. The moon can fit in this shadow. When the moon moves into the earth's shadow, we have a **lunar eclipse**.

During a lunar eclipse, hardly any sunlight reaches the moon. The moon becomes very dim.

You may ask, "How does the moon receive any sunlight when it is hidden in the earth's shadow?" The answer is that the earth's air "bends" some of the sun's light onto the moon. So, even when the moon is eclipsed, it is not completely blacked out. It just looks dull red.

A lunar eclipse lasts much longer than a solar eclipse. This is because the earth's shadow is very wide where the moon passes. The moon takes a long time to pass through.

From start to finish, a lunar eclipse lasts from three to four hours and sometimes longer.

A lunar eclipse can be seen from more areas of the earth than a solar eclipse. During a solar eclipse, the moon's shadow covers only a small part of the earth. A solar eclipse can be seen only on a small part of the earth. A lunar eclipse is different. During a lunar eclipse, the entire moon is in shadow. It can be seen from any part of the earth that is having night at the time of the eclipse.

Lunar eclipses happen more often than solar eclipses.

Figure A shows a total lunar eclipse. Study it. Then fill in the blanks.

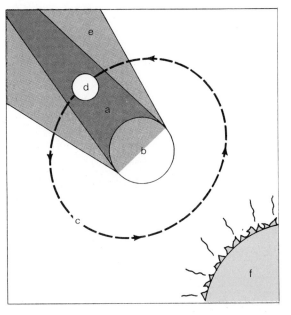

Identify the following by letter:

_f_	**1.**	Sun
_b_	**2.**	Earth
_d_	**3.**	Moon
_c_	**4.**	Moon's orbit
_a_	**5.**	Earth's umbra
_e_	**6.**	Earth's penumbra

Figure A *During a lunar eclipse, the sun, earth and moon line up in a straight line with the earth in the middle.*

There are two kinds of lunar eclipses: <u>total</u> and <u>partial</u>.

The moon looks like this when it is not eclipsed:

A total lunar eclipse looks like this:

A partial lunar eclipse may look like any of these:

7. The moon is in total eclipse when it is in the earth's _____umbra_____ .
   umbra, penumbra

8. The moon is in partial eclipse when it is in the earth's _____penumbra_____ .
   umbra, penumbra

9. When the moon is only partly in the earth's penumbra, the eclipse is

   _____partial_____ .
   total, partial

10. When the moon is partly in the umbra and partly in the penumbra, the eclipse is

    _____partial_____ .
    total, partial

113

THE MOON'S POSITION DURING AN ECLIPSE

Figure G shows the moon in five different positions. What does it look like in each position? Match the positions with the "moons" below.

Figure B

Figure C

Figure D

Figure E

Figure F

Figure G

Answer by letter.

1. In position 1, the moon looks like _____F_____ .

2. In position 2, the moon looks like _____D_____ .

3. In position 3, the moon looks like _____G_____ .

4. In position 4, the moon looks like _____C_____ .

5. In position 5, the moon looks like _____E_____ .

Now answer by number.

6. At which position is the moon not eclipsed at all? _____1_____

7. Why is it not eclipsed? _It is not in the earth's shadow._

8. At which position is the moon totally eclipsed? _____3_____

9. At which positions is the moon partially eclipsed? ___2___ ___4___ ___5___

10. Which one is partially eclipsed the most? _____4_____

114

TRUE OR FALSE

In the space provided, write "true" if the sentence is true. Write "false" if the sentence is false.

False	**1.**	The moon makes its own light.
True	**2.**	The moon reflects the sun's light.
True	**3.**	During a lunar eclipse, the moon is in the earth's shadow.
False	**4.**	During a lunar eclipse, part of the earth is in the moon's shadow.
True	**5.**	During a solar eclipse, part of the earth is in the moon's shadow.
False	**6.**	During a solar eclipse, the moon is in the earth's shadow.
True	**7.**	The whole moon can be covered by the earth's shadow.
False	**8.**	The whole earth can be covered by the moon's shadow.
True	**9.**	The darker part of a shadow is the umbra.
False	**10.**	The darker part of a shadow is the penumbra.

MATCHING

Match each term in Column A with its description in Column B. Write the correct letter in the space provided.

	Column A		**Column B**
d	**1.** umbra	**a)**	lighter part of a shadow
e	**2.** solar eclipse	**b)**	moon is in the earth's shadow
b	**3.** lunar eclipse	**c)**	reflects the sun's light
a	**4.** penumbra	**d)**	darker part of a shadow
c	**5.** moon	**e)**	part of the earth is in the moon's shadow

FILL IN THE BLANK

Complete each statement using a term or terms from the list below. Write your answers in the spaces provided. Some words may be used more than once.

moon
earth's atmosphere
predict
reflects

dull red
does not
longer
sun

earth
larger
disappear
night

1. The moon _____does not_____ make its own light. The moon _____reflects_____ the sun's light.

2. During a lunar eclipse, the moon passes through the shadow of the _____earth_____ .

3. During a lunar eclipse, the _____earth_____ is between the _____sun_____ and the _____moon_____ .

4. During a total lunar eclipse, the moon does not completely _____disappear_____ .

5. A "totally" eclipsed moon is not completely blacked out because the _____earth's atmosphere_____ bends some light onto it.

6. An eclipsed moon looks _____dull red_____ .

7. The earth's shadow is much _____larger_____ than the moon.

8. A lunar eclipse lasts _____longer_____ than a solar eclipse.

9. When a lunar eclipse is taking place, it can be seen from any part of the earth that is having _____night_____ .

10. Scientists can _____predict_____ when and where eclipses will take place.

REACHING OUT

A lunar eclipse can take place only during one moon phase. Which phase is it? Why?

A full moon is the only phase of the moon where the earth is between the moon and the sun. This is the set up needed for a lunar eclipse.

What causes tides?

20

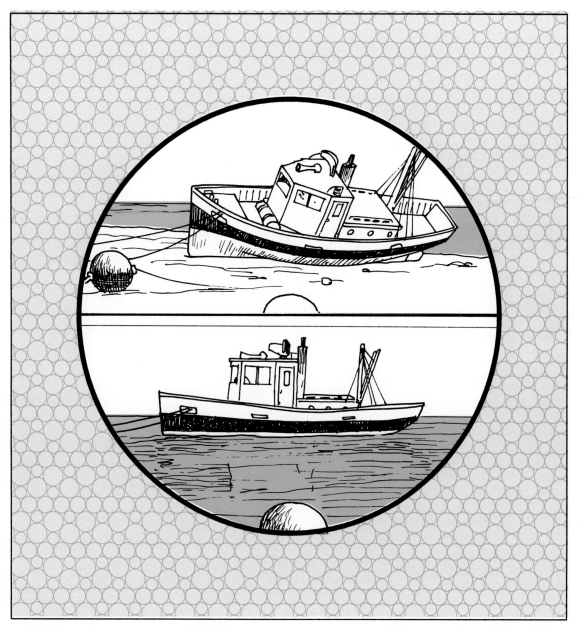

high tide: time of high water level
low tide: time of low water level
neap [NEEP] **tide:** tide that is not as high or low as normal tides
spring tide: tide that is higher and lower than normal tides
tide: daily change of the level of ocean water

LESSON 20 | What causes tides?

Have you ever spent a day at the beach? If you have, then you know that the water in the ocean does not stay at one level. At certain times of the day the water is higher than at other times. The water level rises and falls at regular time periods. We call this regular rise and fall of oceans **tides**.

There are **high tides** and **low tides**. Look at Figure A on the facing page. It shows a coastline at low tide. Figure B shows the same coastline at high tide—just a few hours later. Notice the difference in the water level.

Tides do not change suddenly. High tide moves in slowly. Then, after the water reaches its highest point, it moves out slowly. A low tide is followed by a high tide, which is followed by another low tide.

Most seashores have four tides every day—two high tides and two low tides. A change of tide takes about 6 hours and 12 minutes.

What causes tides?

Tides are caused by the pull of gravity by both the moon and the sun. The moon is more important because it is closer to the earth. The moon pulls on the earth with greater force than the sun.

The moon pulls upon the earth's land and water. The pull has hardly any effect upon the land. Rock does not move easily. But, water is different. Water moves <u>very</u> easily. It flows. The pull bulges the water on the part of the earth that is facing the moon. This part of the earth has high tide. There is also high tide on the opposite side of the earth—the side facing away from the moon.

Areas that supplied the water for high tide areas have low tides.

The earth is always rotating. As it turns, different parts face the moon. This causes the tides to keep changing.

Look at Figure A and B. Answer the questions.

Figure A   *Low tide*

Figure B   *High tide*

1. Why is the boat on land in Figure A? _____It is low tide._____

2. About how long did the water take to change from Figure A to Figure B?

    _____6 hours and 12 minutes_____

3. Which figure shows low tide? _____A_____

4. Which figure shows high tide? _____B_____

5. If you were a fisherman, at which tide would you unload your catch? _____low tide_____

6. At which tide would you go to sea again? _____high tide_____

7. How many times a day could you go to sea? _____twice_____

8. How many times a day could you unload your catch? _____twice_____

119

Study the figures. Then answer the questions.

Figure C

Figure D

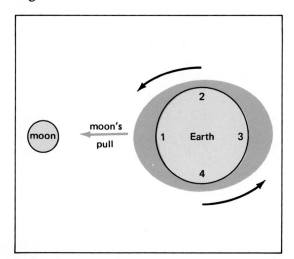

Figure E

If the moon and the sun did not pull on the earth, there would be no tides. The ocean level would be the same everywhere. However, the moon and the sun <u>do</u> pull on the earth.

1. Which one is more important in

   producing tides? ___moon___
   sun, moon

2. Why? The moon is closer to the

   earth.

3. Which side of the earth is facing

   the moon? ___4___
   1, 2, 3, 4

4. Which sides of the earth are

   having high tide? ___4, 2___
   1, 2, 3, 4

5. Which sides are having low tide?

   ___1, 3___
   1, 2, 3, 4

The earth rotates. As it rotates, different parts of the earth face the moon. The tides keep changing.

6. Which sides have high tide now?

   ___1, 3___
   1, 2, 3, 4

7. Which sides have low tide?

   ___2, 4___
   1, 2, 3, 4

8. About how much time has passed between Figures D and E?

   6 hours 12 minutes

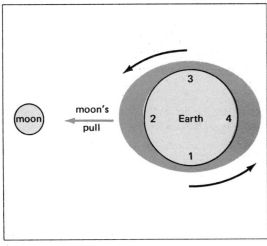

Figure F

9. Now, which sides have high tide?

$$\frac{2, 4}{1, 2, 3, 4}$$

10. About how much time has passed between Figures E and F?

___6 hours 12 minutes___

11. About how much time has passed between Figures D and F?

___12 hours 24 minutes___

12. How long before side 2 has high tide again? ___12 hours 24 minutes___

13. Which other side will have high tide at the same time? ___4___

14. How long before side 3 has low tide again? ___6 hours, 12 minutes___

15. Which other side will have low tide at the same time? ___1___

TWO SPECIAL TIDES

The chief cause of tides is the moon. But the sun also has an effect on tides. Its effect is less. This is because the sun is so far away. Its pull upon the earth is very weak.

The sun's gravity helps produce two special kinds of tides: spring tides and neap [NEEP] tides.

- Spring tides happen twice a month—at new moon and at full moon. Spring tides produce high tides that are higher than usual. Spring tides produce low tides that are lower than usual.

- Neap tides happen twice a month also but at quarter moons. Neap tides produce moderate tides. That is, tides that are not as high and not as low as usual.

Do the following two exercises. They will help you understand spring and neap tides.

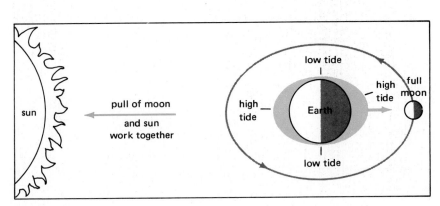

New moon

Figure G

*Full moon
(about 14 days later)*

Figure H

1. At the new moon and at the full moon, the sun, earth, and moon

   _____are_____ in a line.
        are, are not

2. When the sun, earth, and moon are in a line, the pull of gravity upon the earth

   becomes _____stronger_____ .
            stronger, weaker

3. When the sun, earth, and moon are in a line, high tides are _____higher_____
                                                                  higher, lower

   than usual; low tides are _____lower_____ than usual.
                              higher, lower

4. a) What do we call unusually high and low tides? ____spring tides____

   b) How often do they happen? ____twice a month____

5. At which moon phases do spring tides take place? ____new moon____ ____full moon____

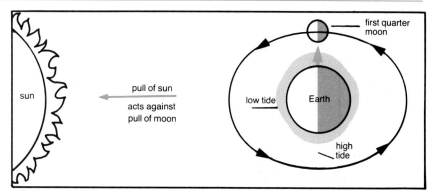

First quarter moon

Figure I

Last quarter moon
(about 14 days later)

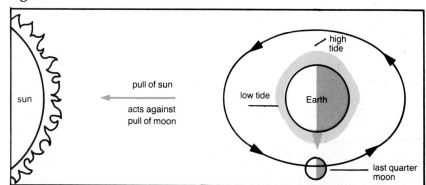

Figure J

6. At quarter moons, the sun, earth, and moon _____ *are not* _____ in a line.
    are, are not

7. At quarter moons, the moon and sun are at right angles. Which of the following is

    a right angle? _____ *c* _____

8. When the moon and sun are at right angles, the gravity pull upon the earth

    becomes _____ *weaker* _____ .
    stronger, weaker

9. When the moon and sun are at right angles, tides are _____ *not very high and not very low* _____ .
    extra high and extra low, not very high
    and not very low

10. Tides that are not very high and not very low are _____ *moderate* _____ tides.
    extreme, moderate

11. a) What do we call moderate tides? _____ *neap* _____

    b) How often do they happen? _____ *twice a month* _____

12. At which moon phases do neap tides take place? _____ *quarter moons* _____

123

WHICH PHASE?

Name the phases of the moon below each picture.

Figure K

Figure L

Figure M

Figure N

1. _New Moon_   2. _First Quarter_   3. _Full Moon_   4. _Last Quarter_

Six events are listed below. Name the phases at which each takes place.

5. Sun, earth and moon are in a line _New Moon_ _Full Moon_

6. Sun, earth, and moon form a right angle _First Quarter_ _Last Quarter_

7. Extra high and extra low tides _New Moon_ _Full Moon_

8. Moderate tides _First Quarter_ _Last Quarter_

9. Spring tides _New Moon_ _Full Moon_

10. Neap tides _First Quarter_ _Last Quarter_

MATCHING

Match each term in Column A with its description in Column B. Write the correct letter in the space provided.

	Column A	Column B
b	1. spring tide	a) time of high water level
e	2. low tide	b) tide that is higher or lower than normal tides
c	3. gravity	c) force of attraction between objects
a	4. high tide	d) tide that is not as high or low as normal tides
d	5. neap tide	e) time of low water level

What is the solar system? | 21

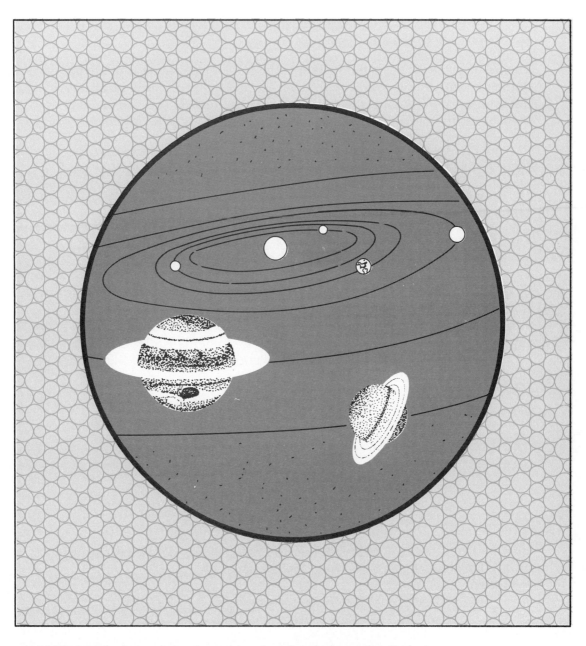

asteroids [AST-uh-roydz]: large chunks of rock that orbit the sun
meteoroid [MEE-tee-or-oyd]: piece of rock or metal that orbits the sun
orbit: curved path of the one object around another object in space
satellite [SAT-uh-lite]: natural or artificial object orbiting a body in space

LESSON 21 | What is the solar system?

Everywhere you look today, you see the word "solar". Solar energy. Solar power. What exactly does the word "solar" mean? "Solar" means "of, or relating to the sun."

The solar system, then, is the system of the SUN. This system is made up of the sun and all the objects that travel around the sun. These **satellites** [SAT-uh-lites] of the sun travel in "paths" called **orbits**. They are held in their orbits by the sun's gravity.

PLANETS   Except for the sun itself, planets are the largest objects in the solar system. Nine planets orbit the sun. One of them is our own home, planet Earth.

MOONS   Most planets have moons. Moons orbit the planets.

ASTEROIDS   Asteroids [AST-uh-roydz] are large chunks of rock. Most asteroids are found in a "belt" between the planets Mars and Jupiter.

COMETS   Comets are made up of rocks, dust and ice. A comet has a small "head" but a very long "tail." The tail extends millions of miles into space — and it points away from the sun. Comets travel around the sun in long elliptical orbits. The most famous comet is Halley's Comet. It takes Halley's Comet 76 years to complete one trip around the sun.

METEROIDS   Meteroids [MEE-tee-or-oyds] are small bits of rock. Most are as small as a grain of sand. Some, however, are as large as boulders. Billions and billions of meteoroids are scattered throughout the solar system.

When a meteoroid enters the earth's atmosphere, friction causes the meteor to glow brightly. It seems to "burn up" as the rock changes it to a gas. While it is "burning up" it is called a meteor or a shooting star. We see it as a bright trail or streak of light in the night sky.

Most meteors burn up completely in the atmosphere. A few reach the earth's surface. A meteor that has reached the earth's surface is called a meteorite.

Study the figure. Then fill in the second column of the chart, listing the planets in order. Start with the planet closest to the sun.

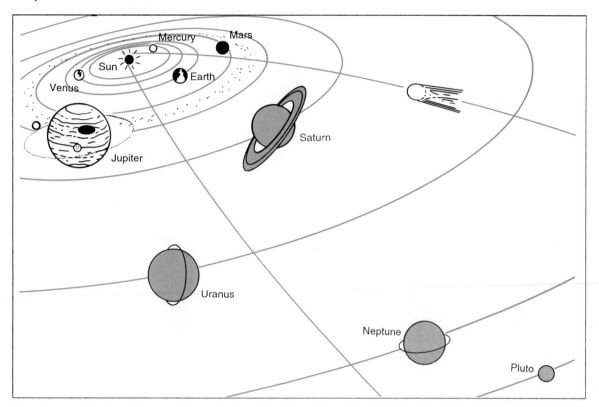

Figure A

Order of Planets from the Sun		
1.	(closest)	Mercury
2.		Venus
3.		Earth
4.		Mars
5.		Jupiter
6.		Saturn
7.		Uranus
8.		Neptune
9.	(farthest)	Pluto

Figure B

Figure B shows the relative sizes of all the planets. Study the figure. Then fill in the second column of the chart listing the planets according to their size. Start with the largest planet.

Planet Size		
1.	(largest)	Jupiter
2.		Saturn
3.		Uranus
4.		Neptune
5.		Earth
6.		Venus
7.		Mars
8.		Mercury
9.	(smallest)	Pluto

Use the figure to answer the following questions.

1. What do the white spheres near the planet stand for? _____Moons_____

2. Only two planets have <u>no</u> moons. Name them. _____Mercury_____

   _____Venus_____

3. Two planets have only <u>one</u> moon each. Name them. _____Earth_____

   _____Pluto_____

4. Which planet has two moons? _____Mars_____

5. Which two planets have the <u>most</u> moons? _____Jupiter_____ _____Saturn_____

6. Which planets have <u>rings</u>? _____Jupiter_____ _____Saturn_____

   _____Uranus_____ _____Neptune_____

7. The four planets closest to the sun are called the <u>inner planets</u>. Name the inner

   planets. _____Mercury_____ _____Venus_____ _____Earth_____

   _____Mars_____

8. The five planets farthest from the sun are called the <u>outer planets</u>. Name the outer

   planets. _____Jupiter_____ _____Saturn_____ _____Venus_____

   _____Neptune_____ _____Pluto_____

FILL IN THE BLANK

Complete each statement using a term or terms from the list below. Write your answers in the spaces provided. Some words may be used more than once.

moons	comet	planets
Jupiter	solar system	Pluto
satellite	sun	Uranus
asteroids	Saturn	

1. The sun and all the space bodies that orbit the sun make up the
   ___solar system___ .

2. The largest objects that orbit the sun are called ___planets___ .

3. The objects that orbit most <u>planets</u> are called ___moons___ .

4. The rocks that form a "belt" between Mars and Jupiter are called
   ___asteroids___ .

5. A ___comet___ is made up of small bits of rock, dust, and ice.

6. A comet orbits the ___sun___ .

7. The planets with rings are ___Jupiter___ , ___Saturn___ , and
   ___Uranus___ .

8. The largest planet is ___Jupiter___ .

9. The planet farthest from the sun is ___Pluto___ .

10. Any space object that orbits another space object is called a ___satellite___ .

TRUE OR FALSE

In the space provided, write "true" if the sentence is true. Write "false" if the sentence is false.

___False___ 1. The stars are part of our solar system.

___True___ 2. The planets are satellites of the sun.

___True___ 3. The Asteroid Belt is located between Mars and Jupiter.

___False___ 4. Saturn is the only planet with rings.

___False___ 5. All planets have moons.

What are the features of the sun?

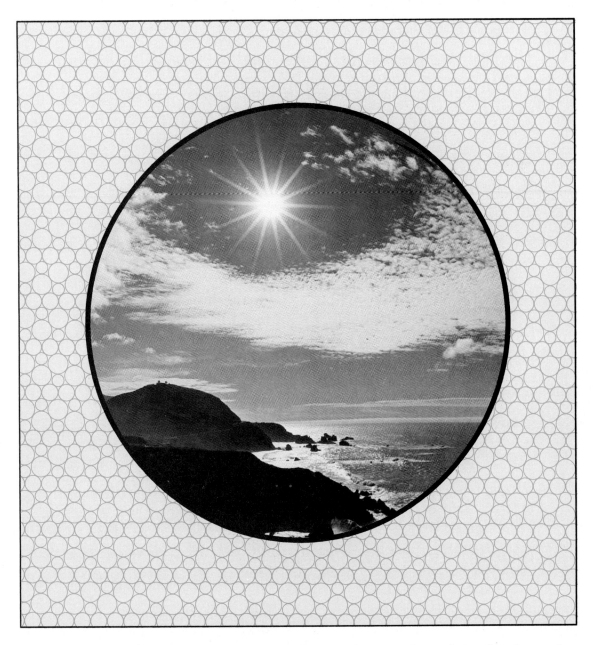

chromosphere [KROH-muh-sfeer]:   layer of the sun's atmosphere above the photosphere
corona [kuh-ROH-nuh]:   outer layer of the sun's atmosphere
photosphere [FOH-tuh-sfeer]:   inner layer of the sun's atmosphere

LESSON 22 | What are the features of the sun?

The sun rises every morning, passes overhead, and sets every evening. The sun is part of our lives. What's more, the sun is essential to our lives. Without the sun there would be no life on earth.

The sun warms the earth. Without the sun the temperature of the earth would be several hundred degrees below zero. Plants get their energy from the sun. Animals get their energy from eating plants or eating animals that eat plants. Without the sun, all plants would soon die, and eventually, we would too.

We need the sun to survive. What do we know about the sun?

The sun is made up of gases only. It is much too hot for there to be solids or liquids. The sun is about three quarters hydrogen and about one quarter helium. There is a relatively tiny amount of other elements in the sun.

Like the earth, the sun is made up of several layers. They are:

CORE The core is the innermost and hottest layer of the sun. The temperature there is about 15 million degrees Celsius (27 million degrees Fahrenheit). The sun's energy is produced in the core.

RADIATION ZONE (4,500,000°C; 8,100,000°F) The radiation zone surounds the core. Solar energy (light) produced in the core moves outward through this section.

CONVECTION ZONE (1,100,000°C; 1,980,000°F) Huge streams of bubbling gases circulate in this layer of the sun. This circulation transfers the heat generated inside the sun at the sun's surface.

PHOTOSPHERE (5,700°C; 10,300°F) The glowing gases in the photosphere [FOH-tuh-sfeer] light the solar system. The photosphere is the part of the sun we see.

The sun is very very bright. Unless you have very special filters, you should never look directly at the sun. Looking at the sun can cause permanent eye damage, even blindness.

There are other ways to study the sun, SO DON'T DO IT!

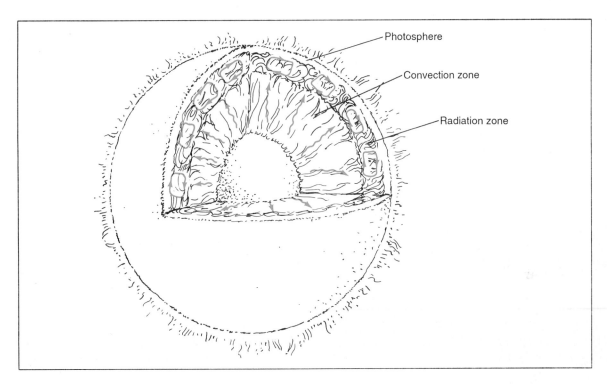

Figure A *The layers of the sun*

Figure B *How to study the sun safely*

Figure C

Figure D *Total Solar Eclipse*

The photosphere is the sun's "surface." Above the photosphere is the sun's atmosphere.

The sun's atmosphere is divided into two layers. The **chromosphere** [KROH-muh-sfeer] is the layer closest to the photosphere. Above the chromosphere is the **corona** [kuh-ROH-nuh].

The chromosphere and corona usually cannot be seen from earth because the sun is so bright.

However, during a solar eclipse, the light from the rest of the sun is blocked out. Therefore the corona and chromosphere can be seen quite easily.

Figure E *Sunspots*

Figure F *Solar Flare*

Sunspots are dark patches of gases in the photosphere. They look dark because they are "cooler" than the gases around them. But they are still very hot — about 3,500°C.

Sunspots are magnetic "storms" and have strong magnetic fields. They usually occur in pairs, and may last from a few days to several weeks before disappearing.

The number of sunspots increase and then decrease in a regular pattern. This is called the sunspot cycle. One sunspot cycle takes about 11 years.

Sometimes, at the peak of a sunspot cycle, tremendous explosions of solar gases take place near sunspots. The eruption of these gases out of the photosphere are called solar flares.

Solar flares shoot atomic particles and radiation into space. Some reach the earth's atmosphere. They interfere with radio communications. Solar flares even affect the weather.

FILL IN THE BLANK

Complete each statement using a term or terms from the list below. Write your answers in the spaces provided.

blindness	photosphere	permanent	gases
chromosphere	sunspots	convection zone	core
radiation zone	weather	total solar eclipse	energy
radio communication	layers	see	corona

1. Looking directly at the sun can cause ____permanent____ eye damage and even ____blindness____ .

2. The sun is divided into ____layers____ of ____gases____ .

3. The innermost section of the sun is the ____core____ . This is where the sun produces its ____energy____ .

4. Solar energy is transferred outward from the core through the ____radiation zone____ .

5. The ____convection zone____ transfer solar energy to the sun's surface.

6. The sun's surface is called the ____photosphere____ . This is the layer we can ____see____ .

7. The layers of the sun's atmosphere are the ____corona____ , and the ____chromosphere____ .

8. The chromosphere and the corona can be seen with the unaided eye only during a ____total solar eclipse____ .

9. Patches of less hot gases in the photosphere are called ____sunspots____ .

10. Sunspots affect ____weather____ and ____radio communication____ .

REACHING OUT

Suppose the number of sunspots was low in 1988. When will the next period of low sunspot activity occur? Why? ____The next period of low sunspot activity will occur in 1999 because that is eleven years after the last period of low activity in 1988.____

What are the inner planets?

23

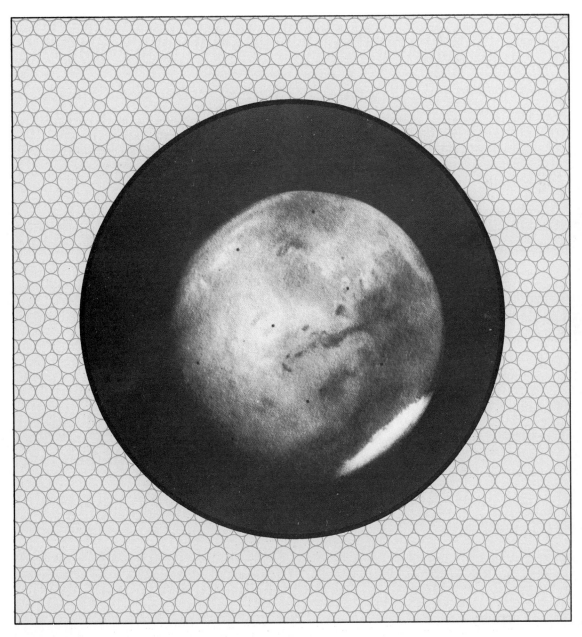

inner planets: the four planets closest to the sun
terrestrial [tuh-RES-tree-uhl] **planets:** planets that are similar to Earth in their size and composition

LESSON 23 | What are the inner planets?

The four planets closest to the sun are called the **inner planets.** The inner planets are similar in a number of ways. The inner planets are also called the **terrestrial** [tuh-RES-tree-uhl] **planets**. Terrestrial means "like the Earth."

The terrestrial plants are relatively small compared to the other planets in the solar system. Unlike the outer planets, they have very little hydrogen and helium. Instead, they are made mostly of rock and iron.

Everything in the solar system formed out of the same mixture of interstellar matter. This interstellar matter was mostly hydrogen and helium. What happened to the hydrogen and helium on the inner planets?

Scientists believe it simply blew away. The inner planets are much smaller than the outer planets. Therefore, the pull of gravity on the inner planets is much smaller. Hydrogen and helium are very light. It takes a strong pull to keep them around a planet. The inner planets did not have a strong enough pull.

Instead, the hydrogen and helium floated out into space. There, particles being shot off from the sun pushed the hydrogen and helium out of the solar system.

Figure A

Mercury is the planet closest to the sun. It is about one third the size of earth and is only one twentieth as massive.

Mercury has no moons and is very similar to Earth's moon. Like the Moon, Mercury has virtually no atmosphere and is heavily cratered.

Mercury rotates on its axis once every 59 days. Since it is closer to the sun than any of the other planets, Mercury takes less time to go around the sun than any other planet. It only takes Mercury 88 days to go all the way around the sun.

The rate of rotation and revolution on Mercury act together to give every place on Mercury 88 days of daylight followed by 88 days of darkness. This causes huge differences in daytime and nighttime temperatures on Mercury. The temperature on Mercury during the day is about 400 degrees Celsius (750°F). At night, the temperature is about 180 degrees below zero Celsius (-290°F). That's quite a change!

The *Mariner 10* spacecraft flew past Mercury three times in 1974 and 1975. This is the only spacecraft to ever visit Mercury. Figure A shows a picture of the planet which was made by putting many detailed photos together.

Figure B

Venus has nearly the same size and mass as Earth. It is often referred to as Earth's sister world.

Venus takes 225 days to go around the sun. Venus rotates very slowly and in the opposite direction of most of the other planets. Scientists believe that Venus once rotated at the same rate that it revolved around the sun, once every 225 days. It always had the same side towards the sun. Earth, however, pulls on Venus as well and Venus now spins so that when it is closest to Earth, it always has the same side facing Earth.

Venus is closer to the sun. If you guessed that Venus is warmer than the earth, you would be right. But the fact that Venus is closer to the sun is only part of the reason that it is so warm. The atmosphere of Venus has a lot of carbon dioxide in it. Carbon dioxide acts like a one way door. The carbon dioxide lets the warmth of the sun reach the surface of Venus very easily. It does not, however, let that heat escape into space very easily. Instead, Venus has gotten warmer and warmer, like you do under a blanket. The temperature on Venus is about 480 degrees Celsius (900°F).

Furthermore, Venus's atmosphere is so thick that the spacecraft that have orbited it have not been able to photograph the surface. Instead, radar is used to map the surface. *Magellan* is a radar mapping space probe that is currently mapping the surface.

Figure C

Earth is your home. It is the home of your family, the home of your friends, the home of everyone you know. Only a few people (astronauts and cosmonauts) have ever left Earth.

We do not usually think of Earth as a planet. It's kind of like not seeing a forest because of the trees. We are so close to Earth (it's right beneath our feet) that we do not recognize it as a planet. It is a planet, and as our home world, it is very important to us.

Earth is the only planet in the solar system we know that has living things on it. There are several reasons why this is so.

The temperatures on Earth are just right for living things to have formed several million years ago, and for living things to survive today.

The temperature on Earth is important for another reason. Water is a liquid on Earth. On planets closer to the sun, the temperatures are higher than Earth's and water is found only as a gas. On planets farther away from the sun than Earth, it is colder and water is found only as a solid.

On Earth, however, we have oceans of liquid water, and liquid water is needed by living things. The next time you go outside, consider how lucky you are to have Earth for your home.

Figure D   **Figure E**

Mars is about half the size of Earth and is twice the size of the moon. A red dust covers the planet and you can recognize Mars in the sky because of its reddish color.

People have often wondered about Mars. In 1877, an Italian astronomer named Giovanni Schiaparelli noticed dark markings he called canali, which means "channels." The American astronomer Percival Lowell interpreted Shiaparelli's writings to mean that Mars had canals like the canals on Earth. Lowell thought that these canals must have been created by Martians, intelligent beings on Mars. For half a century, people would imagine little green men and women lived on Mars.

In fact, when a fictional story about an invasion from Mars was broadcast on the radio in the 1930s, many people thought it was real!

We now know that there are no little green men and women on Mars, but the possibility that there could be life still exists. Water is a necessary ingredient in the development of life on a planet, and Mars once had a great deal of water. Even though the planet is now very dry, if there had been life on Mars when the planet had more water, the life forms could have evolved to live in the present dry climate.

In 1976, two *Viking* spacecraft landed on Mars. One of their main objectives was to check the Martian surface for life. They found many of the necessary ingredients for life but no evidence that there was actually anything alive on the planet.

FILL IN THE BLANK

Complete each statement using a term or terms from the list below. Write your answers in the spaces provided. Some words may be used more than once.

Mercury   Earth   liquid
Venus   Mars   *Viking* spacecraft
terrestrial   *Mariner 10* moon

1. _____Mercury_____ is the planet closest to the sun.

2. Mercury is similar to Earth's _____moon_____ .

3. Mercury, Venus, Earth and Mars are _____terrestrial_____ planets.

4. _____Earth_____ and _____Venus_____ are about the same size.

5. _____*Mariner 10*_____ was a spacecraft that studied Mercury.

6. _____Venus_____ has a very thick atmosphere.

7. _____Earth_____ is the only planet known to have life on it.

8. On Earth, water is usually found as a _____liquid_____ .

9. _____Mars_____ is a red planet.

10. In 1975, two _____*Viking* spacecraft_____ landed on _____Mars_____ .

MATCHING

Match each term in Column A with its description in Column B. Write the correct letter in the space provided.

Column A		Column B
__c__	1. *Magellan*	a) half the size of Earth
__b__	2. *Viking*	b) studied Mars
__d__	3. *Mariner 10*	c) studying Venus
__e__	4. Venus	d) studied Mercury
__a__	5. Mars	e) same size as Earth

Use the clues to complete the crossword puzzle.

	¹S	²A	T	U	R	N			³M	O	O	N	
		S							E				
		T			⁴J				R				
⁵M		E			U				C				
⁶E	A	R	T	H		⁷P	L	U	T	⁸O			
T		O			I		R		R				
E		I			T		Y		B		⁹C		
O		D			E				I		O		
R		¹⁰S	O	L	A	R	S	Y	S	T	E	M	
O											E		
I											T		
D													

Clues

Across

1. First planet known to have rings
3. Body that orbits a planet
6. The planet we live on
7. Farthest planet from the sun
10. The sun and everything that travels around it

Down

2. Found in a belt between Mars and Jupiter
3. Planet nearest to the sun
4. Largest planet
5. "Shooting star"
8. "Paths" in which objects travel around the sun
9. Travels in long, cigar-shaped path around the sun

What are the outer planets?

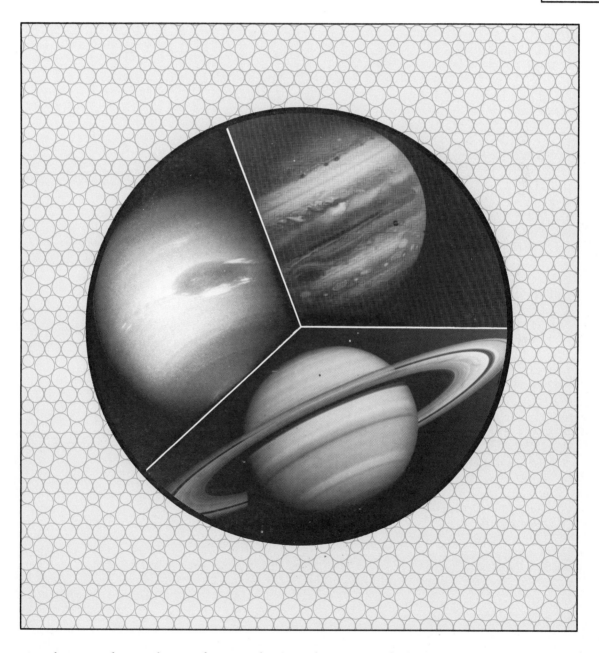

gas giants: planets that are large and primarily composed of gases

LESSON 24 | What are the outer planets?

Beyond the orbit of Mars lies an asteroid belt that mark the boundary between the inner planets and the outer planets. The inner planets are generally the same size and made of the same rocky material.

In general, the outer planets are totally different from the inner planets.

Jupiter, Saturn, Uranus, and Neptune are gas giants. The smallest of the four, Neptune, is 60 times the size of Earth. As their name suggests, gas giants are primarily made of gases. They are very similar to stars that never started shining. In fact, some scientists suggest that if Jupiter had been a few times larger, it would have become a star.

The one outer planet that is not a gas giant is Pluto, the small planet that belongs in a class by itself.

Figure A *Jupiter, Io, and Europa*

Jupiter, like the other planets, is named after a mythological Roman god. The mythological Jupiter was king of the gods and Jupiter is king of the planets. Jupiter is the largest planet in the solar system.

The most prominent feature of Jupiter is its red spot. This storm in its atmosphere has been raging for as long as we have been able to see it. With the exception of the red spot, Jupiter's atmosphere can be described as a number of bands stretching around the planet.

Jupiter has four very large moons that can be seen with even the weakest telescopes. These moons, discovered by Galileo, are called the Galilean satellites. The giant planet also has about a dozen smaller moons.

Io, the smallest moon, is a fiery world with very active volcanos, caused by Jupiter's gravitational pull on the moon. Europa is an extremely smooth moon which has an icy surface. Caliosto and Ganymede are two moons about the size of Mercury. Calisto is very similar to Mercury and Earth's moon in that it is covered with craters. Ganymede is not completely understood since it is largely made of ice. From a geological perspective, ice is a very complex material.

Almost all we know about Jupiter was learned by the *Voyager 1* and *Voyager 2* flybys. These two spacecraft took a tour of the outer solar system in the 1970s and 1980s and Jupiter was the first planet they encountered. The cameras on the *Voyager* spacecraft took pictures far, far better than any that could be taken from Earth. The spacecraft also carried other equipment which performed a number of other experiments as the spacecraft flew past Jupiter.

One of the most important discoveries made by Voyager spacecraft was that Jupiter has a ring around it. This ring is much fainter than the one around Saturn or Neptune. The discovery of a ring around Jupiter showed that most gas giants in the solar system have rings.

Figure B

Saturn is known as the ringed planet. From Earth, it is relatively easy to see four distinct rings through a telescope. When *Voyager* reached Saturn, however, no one was prepared for what it found. There were thousands of rings! Almost too many to count. The rings are made of dust and rocks of various sizes.

Voyager 1 flew past Jupiter in March, 1979. The gravity of Jupiter then catapulted it towards Saturn, which it reached in November 1980. This push allowed *Voyager 1* to reach Saturn much more quickly using far less energy. *Voyager 2* was pushed by Jupiter in the same manner. What's more, Saturn's gravitational pull pushed *Voyager 2* on to Uranus. Uranus in turn, pushed *Voyager 2* on towards Neptune.

Scientists were able to plot this course for the *Voyager* spacecraft because the planets were on a special alignment. This alignment only happens about once every two hundred years.

Saturn has a large number of moons. Titan, the largest of these moons is bigger than the planet Mercury. Titan is both larger and colder than Earth's moon. Titan's temperature and mass allow it to have a thick atmosphere. In fact, it has more of an atmosphere than Mars or Earth. Like Earth, Titan's atmosphere is mostly made up of nitrogen. The conditions on Titan are very similar to what existed on Earth a long time ago, with one important exception. Titan is much colder than Earth. The temperature on Titan is 177 degrees below zero Celsius (-180°F). Still, studying Titan may help us understand the Earth's own history.

Figure C

For many years, Uranus and Neptune have been thought of as twins. Both planets are roughly the same size, with a diameter of about 50,000 kilometers. They both also have a deep blue color, like the sky on a very clear day. However, as we have learned more about these two worlds, some differences have been discovered between these two brothers.

Uranus was discovered in 1781. Five years after the United States had declared independence from Britain, an amateur astronomer named William Herschel was using a six inch telescope to study some stars. One of the stars appeared as a disk on his telescope rather than a point of light. He watched it over a period of many nights and discovered it moved with respect to the other stars. What Hershel had discovered was not a star but was a planet, what we now call the planet Uranus.

On March 10, 1977, Jim Elliot, a professional astronomer, studied Uranus as it passed in front of a bright star. Astronomers can tell a lot about a planet by watching it eclipse a star. The light from the star was blocked as the planet passed in front of the star. Furthermore, the light was blocked out just before and just after it passed by the planet. The cause of this was a set of rings that were too small to be seen from Earth. Until this discovery, Saturn was the only planet we knew that had rings. Now we know that several planets have them.

When *Voyager* 2 visited Uranus, its cameras showed that the atmosphere of the planet is very smooth, unlike the storms and bands visible in the other gas giants.

Figure D

Once Uranus had been discovered, astronomers rushed to plot and calculate its orbit around the sun. They could not figure it out. Even after calculating the effect of all the other planets on Uranus, it still did not follow the predicted orbit. Scientists suggested that there must be another planet farther out than Uranus that had not been discovered. They then set out to calculate where it would be. A search was made.

On September 23, 1846 Neptune was discovered almost exactly where John Couch Adams and Urbain Jean Joseph LeVerrier, two mathematicians, had predicted it would be found. This was a tremendous triumph for science and mathematics.

While Neptune resembles Uranus in its color, its atmosphere resembles Jupiter's atmosphere. Instead of a large red spot, Neptune has a large dark spot.

After rings were discovered on Uranus and Jupiter, scientists wondered if Neptune had rings. A search for rings around Neptune was undertaken. The same process that found the rings around Uranus was used, but was not effective. Scientists would sometimes find the light blocks on one but not the other. Since rings go around both sides of the planet, they should block the light on both sides

Voyager 2 solved the controversy by clearly showing that Neptune had rings. An individual ring was sometimes thicker on one side than it was on the other. Scientists on Earth could only detect the thicker part of the rings.

In 1610, Galileo first saw the rings around Saturn. For the next 367 years, people believed that Saturn was the only planet that had a ring system. In thirteen years, from 1977 to 1990, scientists have learned that all the gas giants have rings. That is an amazing discovery in such a short period of time.

Figure E

After the discovery of Neptune astronomers continually wondered whether there could be a ninth planet. Sometimes, searches were made for such an object. One search was carried out at Lowell observatory, founded by the same Percival Lowell who thought there were canals on Mars. Clyde Tombaugh, an assistant at the observatory, would study two pictures of the same section of the sky taken at different times. He would look to see whether any object in the picture had moved. On February 18, 1930, Tombaugh discovered Pluto.

Pluto usually is the farthest planet from the sun. Its orbit is very elliptical and it crosses the orbit of Neptune. Right now it is closer to the sun than Neptune and it will be until 1999.

We do not know very much about Pluto since it is so far away and no spacecraft have visited it. Pluto is the smallest planet in the solar system and is slightly smaller than the Moon. It has a moon of its own named Charon and a very thin atmosphere made mostly of methane.

Since it is so far from the sun, Pluto is very cold. It usually is about 225° below zero Celsius (-373°F) on Pluto.

Some scientists do not think that Pluto should be considered a planet. It is very different than all the other planets in the solar system. It is most like some of the moons of the gas giants.

Unfortunately, there are no plans to send a spacecraft to Pluto, even though it is the only planet that has not yet been visited. For the time being, at least, much about Pluto will remain a mystery.

FILL IN THE BLANK

Complete each statement using a term or terms from the list below. Write your answers in the spaces provided. Some words may be used more than once.

Voyager 1	Jupiter	Neptune	gas giants
Voyager 2	Saturn	Uranus	Pluto

1. _____Jupiter_____ is the largest planet.

2. The first planet known to have rings was _____Saturn_____ .

3. _____Neptune_____ and _____Uranus_____ are bluish in color.

4. Neptune, Uranus, Jupiter and Saturn are _____gas giants_____ .

5. _____Neptune_____ is the farthest planet from the sun right now.

6. _____Pluto_____ is usually the farthest planet from the sun.

7. _____Voyager 1_____ and _____Voyager 2_____ are spacecraft that flew by

   Jupiter and Saturn.

8. _____Voyager 2_____ also flew by Uranus and Neptune.

9. _____Pluto_____ is the smallest planet.

10. _____Pluto_____ was not visited by Voyager 1 or Voyager 2.

MATCHING

Match each term in Column A with its description in Column B. Write the correct letter in the space provided.

	Column A	Column B
__c__	1. Io	a) moon of Pluto
__a__	2. Charon	b) moon of Saturn
__b__	3. Titan	c) volcanic moon of Jupiter
__e__	4. Triton	d) four Galilean moons
__d__	5. Ganymede, Calisto, Europa, and Io	e) moon of Neptune

What are stars?

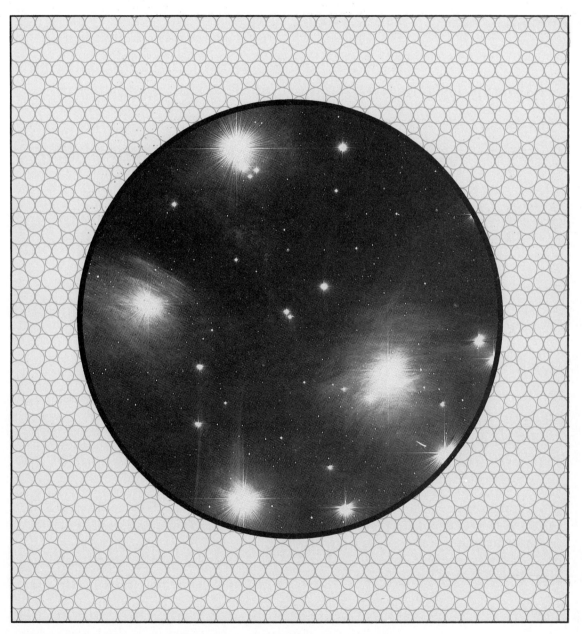

absolute [AB-suh-loot] **magnitude:** true brightness of a star
apparent [uh-PER-unt] **magnitude:** brightness a star seems to have
magnitude [MAG-nuh-tood]: star brightness

LESSON 25 | What are stars?

Our sun is a star. In fact, our sun is a very average star. There are billions and billions of stars in the galaxy. Some are as bright as the sun. Some are much, much brighter. Why, then, does the sun appear to be so much larger and brighter than all the other stars? Because it is so much closer to Earth than the next nearest star. The sun's brightness is **apparent brightness**!

If something is hot enough, it will "glow." It will give off light. Stars are made up of very hot gases. "Starlight"—the light given off by stars—is the light given off by the very hot gases that make up the stars.

Without a telescope, stars look like tiny points of white light. Actually, light from different stars can be different in two important ways—color and brightness.

COLOR   When viewed through a telescope, stars have different colors. The color of a star depends on its temperature. The hottest stars are bluish white. The coolest stars are reddish-orange. "Medium-hot" stars are yellow.

BRIGHTNESS   There are two "kinds" of brightness—true brightness and apparent brightness. True brightness depends on size and temperature. The bigger and hotter an object is, the brighter it will actually be.

Apparent brightness depends mostly on distance. For example, a dim light that is close can seem brighter than a bright light that is farther away. Thus, a dim star that is close to Earth will appear brighter than a bright star that is farther away.

Star brightness is called **magnitude** [MAG-nuh-tood]. The true brightness of a star is called **absolute** [AB-suh-loot] **magnitude**. But, this is not the brightness we see when we look up at the stars. The stars that appear brightest are those closest to Earth. This brightness is called **apparent** [uh-PER-unt] **magnitude**.

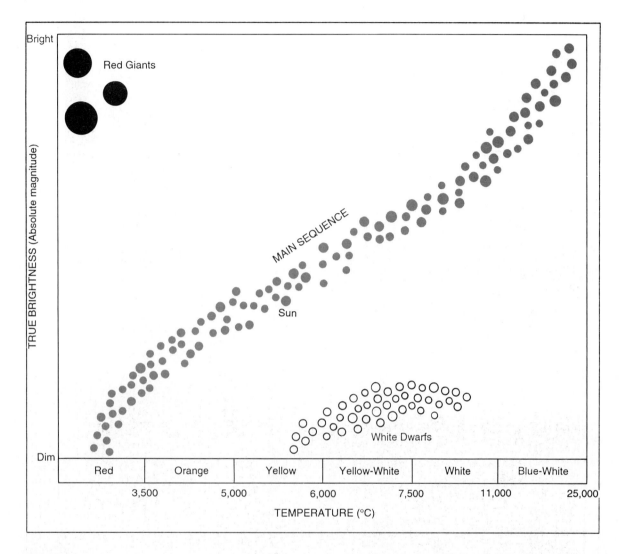

Figure A

Look at Figure A. For the stars in the main sequence, the brighter a star is, the hotter it is as well. There is a relationship between the color of a star and its brightness.

The scientists who study stars have determined that while stars are <u>not</u> alive they <u>do</u> have a life cycle similar to the life cycle of people. When stars are "born," they are dim, cool, and red. As stars age, they get brighter and hotter.

The place of a star on the main sequence is determined by its age. The stars in the bottom left corner are the youngest and the stars in the upper right corner are the oldest.

When stars get very old, they stay very bright, but they get much cooler and larger. They become red giants. Red giants are very old stars.

Some red giants, the smaller ones, eventually shrink and get dimmer, but they get whiter as well. They become white dwarfs.

Therefore, where a star is on this graph tells us how old the star is.

Study Figures B and C. Answer the questions.

Figure B

Figure B shows two light bulbs. Both are the same distance from the girl.

1. Which bulb glows more brightly?

   _____ Y _____
   X, Y

2. You would make both bulbs seem

   brighter by moving them

   _____ closer to _____ the girl.
   closer to, farther away from

3. How would you make bulb X seem as bright as bulb Y? List two ways.

   a) __ Move bulb X closer to the girl. __

   _____

   b) __ Move bulb Y farther away __

   __ from the girl. __

Figure C

Figure C shows stars. Stars X and Y seem equally bright. Yet, X really gives off more light than Y.

4. Which star is farther away?

   _____ Y _____
   X, Y

5. Which star is closer? _____ Y _____
   X, Y

156

MATCHING

Match each term in Column A with its description in Column B. Write the correct letter in the space provided.

	Column A		Column B
c	1. star color	a)	a yellow star
d	2. true brightness	b)	stars not on the main sequence
b	3. red giants	c)	depends on temperature
e	4. apparent brightness	d)	absolute magnitude
a	5. the sun	e)	depends on distance

FILL IN THE BLANK

Complete each statement using a term or terms from the list below. Write your answers in the spaces provided. Some words may be used more than once.

blue-white   absolute magnitude   yellow
temperature   the sun   distance
red giants   starlight   hot gases
                                          star

1. Stars are made up of very _____hot gases_____ .

2. Apparent brightness depends mostly on _____distance_____ .

3. The color of the hottest stars is _____blue-white_____ .

4. Large, cool stars that are not on the main sequence are _____red giants_____ .

5. "Medium-hot" stars are _____yellow_____ .

6. Star color depends mostly on _____temperature_____ .

7. _____Starlight_____ is the light given off by stars.

8. The brightest star in our sky is _____the sun_____ .

9. _____Star_____ brightness depends on size and temperature.

10. The true brightness of a star is called _____absolute magnitude_____ .

WORD SEARCH

The list on the left contains words that you have used in this Lesson. Find and circle each word where it appears in the box. The spellings may go in any direction": up, down, left, right, or diagonally.

STARLIGHT
APPARENT
BRIGHTNESS
TEMPERATURE
RED GIANT
SUN
MAGNITUDE
DISTANCE
COLOR
ABSOLUTE

```
P  R  E  A  L  F  C  O  N  T  E  R
S  A  T  T  N  A  I  G  D  E  R  N
M  O  U  S  E  D  O  O  R  M  A  T
A  L  L  W  E  R  T  Y  O  P  S  H
G  R  O  A  N  I  W  A  S  E  L  G
N  A  S  A  L  C  O  L  O  R  X  I
I  M  B  S  O  L  U  R  E  A  E  L
T  I  A  P  P  A  R  E  N  T  O  R
U  N  D  E  R  O  V  E  R  U  P  A
D  I  S  T  A  N  C  E  A  R  S  T
E  X  B  R  I  G  H  T  N  E  S  S
```

How do stars get their energy?

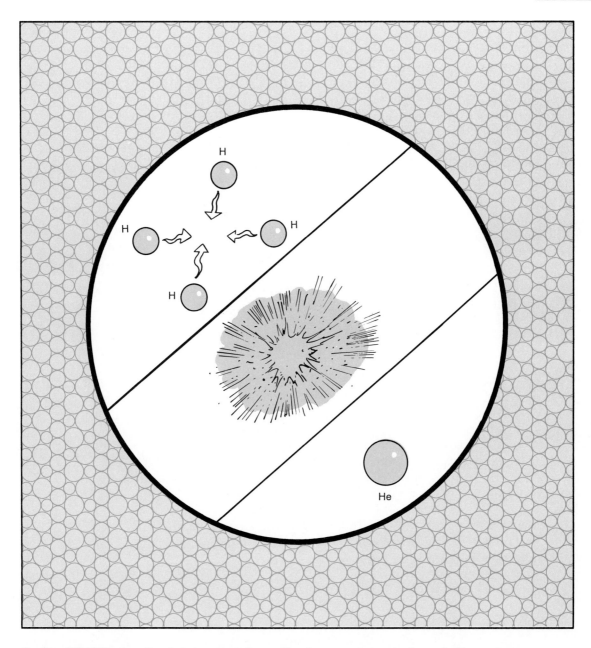

fusion [FYOO-zhun]:   joining together of hydrogen atoms to form helium atoms

LESSON 26 | How do stars get their energy?

What are stars? Most people would say "balls of burning gases." Well, this is not entirely correct. Stars are made up of gases. But they are not burning. They are glowing The gases give off light because they are so hot. In fact, anything that is hot enough glows.

Burning is a kind of chemical reaction. It is the linkup of oxygen with another substance. This linkup is not happening in stars. No burning can take place in stars. There are two reasons:

- Stars do not have enough oxygen.

- Strange as it seems, the stars are just too hot for burning to take place

The reaction that gives the sun its energy is called **nuclear fusion** [FYOO-zhun]. Nuclear fusion joins or fuses the nuclei of atoms. This produces different kinds of atoms.

The Sun is about 70% hydrogen. Part of this hydrogen is changed into helium by fusion.

Four hydrogen atoms fuse together. This produces one helium atom. However, about 1% of the mass of the hydrogen atoms does not become part of the new helium atom. It changes into energy, in the form of heat and light.

Each fusion reaction produces only a small amount of energy. But an enormous number of fusion reactions take place. An enormous amount of hydrogen changes to helium. A great deal of energy is given off.

Every second, about 500 million metric tons of hydrogen change to 495 million metric tons of helium. The remaining 5 million metric tons change to a huge amount of energy.

This is a nuclear equation.

$$4 \text{ H} \xrightarrow{\text{Temperature of millions of degree}} \text{He} + \text{energy}$$

It tells us that four atoms of hydrogen fuse to form one atom of helium—plus ENERGY

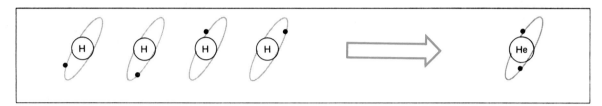

Figure A

Where does this energy come from?

Follow the explanation step-by-step.

* The atomic mass of hydrogen is 1.0081.

* The atomic mass of helium is 4.0039.

Four hydrogen atoms have a mass of 4.0324 atomic mass units (a.m.u.)

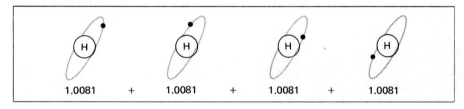

Figure B $4 \times 1.0081 = 4.0324$ a.m.u.

One helium atom has a mass of 4.0039

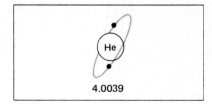

Figure C

We see that one helium atom weighs 0.0285 less than four hydrogen atoms.

$$\begin{array}{r} 4.0324 \text{ a.m.u.} \\ - 4.0039 \text{ a.m.u.} \\ \hline 0.0285 \text{ a.m.u.} \end{array}$$

* It is this 0.0285 a.m.u. of matter that changes to energy.

* This reaction takes place trillions and trillions of times each second and powers stars.

Talk about diets! Every second, 5 million tons of the sun's hydrogen change to energy.

This means that the sun loses 5 million metric tons of mass every second.

How much matter does the sun lose in just one year? One hundred fifty seven trillion, six hundred eighty billion metric tons. (157,680,000,000,000). Larger stars use even more energy!

Will the sun ever be used up? Yes, but not for a long, long time. The sun is so huge that it will keep on giving off heat and light for at least another billion years.

Figure D *Fusion takes place inside the sun's center.*

Hydrogen bombs use fusion energy as well. However, hydrogen bombs release all of their energy in one destructive explosion which lasts only one millionth of a second.

Scientists are trying to create reactors which use fusion energy to produce electricity. They have had some success, but practical uses of fusion energy are a long way off.

Figure E *Hydrogen bomb*

FILL IN THE BLANK

Complete each statement using a term or terms from the list below. Write your answers in the spaces provided.

burning	four	oxygen
helium	nuclear	energy
hydrogen	one	fusion
chemical	nuclei	light

1. Burning is a _____chemical_____ reaction in which _____oxygen_____ links up with another substance.

2. The energy that powers stars is not caused by _____burning_____ .

3. Stars get their energy from _____nuclear_____ reactions.

4. The kind of nuclear reaction that gives stars their energy is called _____fusion_____.

5. Fusion joins the _____nuclei_____ of atoms.

6. The sun is made up mostly of _____hydrogen_____ .

7. Fusion on the sun joins atoms of hydrogen. _____Four_____ hydrogen atoms fuse to form _____one_____ atom of helium.

8. _____Helium_____ is nearly four times heavier than hydrogen.

9. About 1% of the mass of the hydrogen atoms does not become helium atoms. It changes to _____energy_____ .

10. Anything that becomes hot enough gives off _____light_____ .

MATCHING

Match each term in Column A with its description in Column B. Write the correct letter in the space provided.

Column A	Column B
__d__ 1. fuse	a) give the sun its energy
__a__ 2. fusion reactions	b) nearly four times heavier than hydrogen
__c__ 3. hydrogen	c) about 75% of the sun
__e__ 4. sun	d) join
__b__ 5. helium	e) a star

WORD SCRAMBLE

Below are several scrambled words you have used in this Lesson. Unscramble the words and write your answers in the spaces provided.

1. SIFONU   FUSION

2. MILUHE   HELIUM

3. GEENYR   ENERGY

4. RANLUCE   NUCLEAR

5. GRODHENY   HYDROGEN

What are constellations? 27

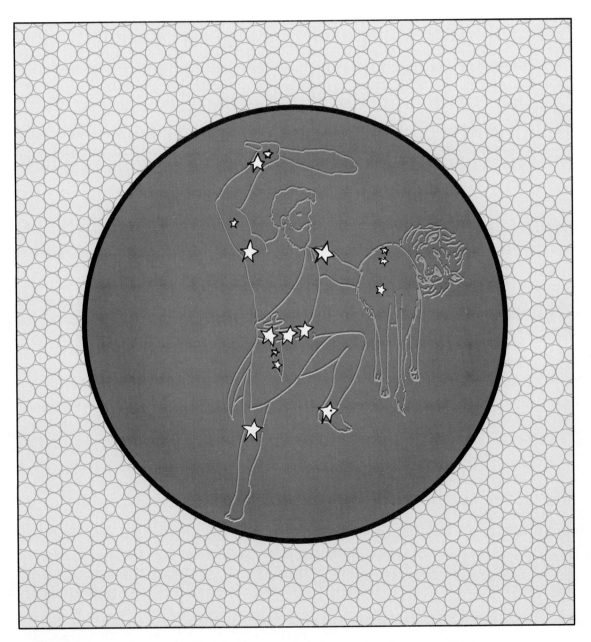

constellation [kon-stuh-LAY-shun]: a group of stars that form a pattern
North Star: Polaris, the star above the north pole
Pole Star: Polaris, the star above the north pole

LESSON 27 | What are constellations?

Have you ever looked at the Big Dipper in the sky? With a little practice, it is fairly easy to find the stars that make up the Big Dipper. Why is this so?

There are seven stars that make up the Big Dipper. These stars form a pattern. Every night, when you look up into the sky, you can see this same pattern. People are good at learning patterns and then recognizing these patterns.

In ancient times, people divided the stars in the sky into different groups called **constellations** [kon-stuh-LAY-shuns]. Each constellation formed a pattern. Different societies had divided the stars up differently. The patterns reminded them of people, animals or things in their world. People would name the constellations after the things the constellations reminded them of. For example, Orion is a group of stars that reminded the ancient Greeks of Orion, the Hunter.

Astronomers today have divided the sky into 88 constellations. Every star in the sky is part of some constellation although only the brightest stars are used to form the patterns the constellation is named after. Astronomers use the names of constellations to help keep track of the stars in the sky.

The stars in a constellation look like they are close to each other as we look at them from earth. However, that does not mean that they really are close to each other. The stars in a constellation are not all the same distance from us. Some stars in a constellation are much closer to us than the other stars in the same constellation.

Figure A *Orion*

Figure B *Casseopia*

Figure C *Ursa Major, the great bear*

Figure D *Ursa Minor, the little bear*

The earth, you know, rotates on its axis. As the earth turns, the sun seems to move across the sky. The earth's rotation makes the stars seem to move across the sky as well. If we took a long exposure picture, we could see the stars trace out lines across the sky. There is one star, however, that does not seem to move across the sky. This star, named Polaris, is directly above the north pole. Like the center of a spinning record or spinning top, Polaris does not seem to move. Because Polaris is above the north pole, it is also called the Pole Star or the North Star.

Figure E

MATCHING

Match each term in Column A with its description in Column B. Write the correct letter in the space provided.

	Column A	Column B
d	1. constellation	a) the hunter
a	2. Orion	b) Pole Star
b	3. Polaris	c) little bear
e	4. sun	d) pattern of stars
c	5. Ursa Minor	e) nearest star

FILL IN THE BLANK

Complete each statement using a term or terms from the list below. Write your answers in the spaces provided. Some words may be used more than once.

stars   patterns   look
Orion   rotates   distance
sun   constellations   North Star
Casseopia   Pole Star   Polaris
north pole

1. People are good at learning to recognize _____patterns_____ .

2. A long time ago people divided the stars into groups called _____constellations_____ .

3. A constellation is made up of a group of _____stars_____ .

4. _____Orion_____ and _____Casseopia_____ are constellations.

5. The stars in a constellation _____look_____ as if they are close to each other.

6. The stars in a constellation are not all the same _____distance_____ from us.

7. The Earth _____rotates_____ on its axis.

8. Because the Earth rotates, the _____sun_____ and _____stars_____ seem

   to move across the sky.

9. _____Polaris_____ does not seem to move across the sky because it is above

   the _____north pole_____ .

10. Polaris is also known as the _____North Star_____ or the _____Pole Star_____ .

REACHING OUT

How could Polaris be useful to a person who is lost? (Hint: why is Polaris called the North

Star?) _____Polaris is always north, so a person looking at Polaris knows which_____

_____direction is north._____

SCIENCE *EXTRA*

Aerospace Technician

Neil Armstrong's "one small step for man, one giant leap for mankind" was not the achievement of just one man. Instead, his first step onto the moon's surface was the result of the labors of thousands and thousands of people. Many of those people were aerospace technicians.

Aerospace technicians built the Saturn 5 rocket which launched Armstrong into space. The technicians also built the capsule and lunar lander that carried him to the moon. They even made the space suit that he wore as he made his historic step.

Aerospace technicians build space probes, satellites, spacecraft and any other equipment that is being used in space.

The conditions in space are so severe that space equipment must be made specifically for these conditions. Even something as simple as a screw must be made of special materials to survive the conditions of outer space.

The equipment aerospace technicians make is very, very complicated.

Therefore, they take special care to make sure that the equipment they make is not defective. If something does not work the way it is supposed to, millions of dollars (even the lives of astronauts) could be lost. For this reason, aerospace technicians are very detail oriented. All work is checked and rechecked to make sure that no mistakes are made.

If, when the equipment is launched, everything functions properly, (which it usually does) aerospace technicians can be proud of the job they have done. All their hard work has paid off.

Aerospace technicians may either work for government agencies like NASA or for private aerospace companies. If you would like to be an aerospace technician, you should study math and science in school. After graduating from high school. you could either go to college and major in science or engineering or go to a technical school.

Aerospace engineering is a career with both personal and financial rewards. It may be the career for you.

What are galaxies?

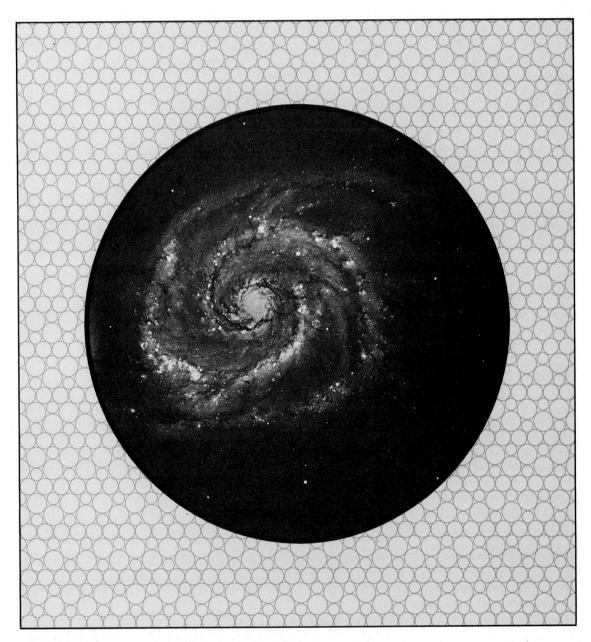

elliptical galaxy: spherical or flattened disk-shaped galaxy
galaxy [GAL-uhk-see]:   large group of stars
irregular galaxy: galaxy with no definite shape
Milky Way galaxy: the galaxy in which the sun is located
spiral galaxy: galaxy with a thick center and flattened arms

LESSON 28 | What are galaxies?

Look up at the sky on a clear night. How many stars can you see? Take a guess. One hundred? One thousand? One million? Without a telescope, about 5,000 stars are visible from Earth. That is, from the entire Earth! Not just from your back yard.

Through a powerful telescope, millions of individual stars can be seen. Does this mean that most of the stars are visible through a telescope? Not at all. There are more stars than we could ever hope to count. There may even be an infinite number of stars.

Stars are not just scattered throughout space. They are sort of bunched together in very large groups or systems, called **galaxies** [GAL-uhk-seez]. Each galaxy contains hundreds of millions of stars. And the galaxies are millions of light-years apart.

There are three main types of galaxies—spiral, elliptical, and irregular.

A **spiral galaxy** looks something like a giant pinwheel. It has a thick center and several "arms" that spiral around the center. The planet Earth is located in a spiral galaxy—the **Milky Way galaxy**. Our sun is one of more than 100 billion stars in this galaxy.

An **elliptical galaxy** looks something like the lens of a magnifying glass. It has no arms, and most of the stars are concentrated near its center.

Irregular galaxies have no definite shape.

Figure A *Spiral galaxy*

Most galaxies are spiral galaxies. Our solar system is in the spiral galaxy called the Milky Way. We are one of the many stars in one of the arms of the Milky Way. We can't take a picture of the entire Milky Way, because we are <u>inside</u> it. However, if you go far away from city lights and look up at a very clear, very dark sky, you can see a band across the sky that glows faintly. That glow is from millions and millions of stars in the Milky Way that are too faint to see.

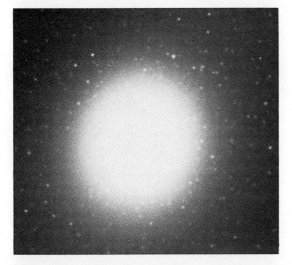

Figure B *Elliptical galaxy*

Elliptical galaxies look like a ball that has been squished. The stars in elliptical galaxies are usually older than the stars in spiral galaxies. Therefore, elliptical galaxies are usually not as bright as spiral galaxies.

Figure C *Irregular galaxy*

Irregular galaxies are the least common type of galaxy. The stars in an irregular galaxy are not arranged evenly so irregular galaxies have no definite shape. Irregular galaxies are smaller and fainter than the other kinds of galaxies.

Figure D

While studying galaxies, Astronomer Edwin Hubble discovered that all galaxies are moving away from each other. This means that the galaxies used to be much closer to each other. At some point a long, long time ago, everything in the universe must have been together at the same place.

Many scientists now believe that about 15 billion years ago, the universe came into being in what scientists call the big bang. This cosmic explosion created all the matter in the universe and the force of the explosions sent the matter off in all directions.

The forces that would have been acting very early in the universe are very different from what we experience in our everyday lives. As a result, scientists do not completely understand how the universe began. There is still much more to learn.

TRUE OR FALSE

In the space provided, write "true" if the sentence is true. Write "false" if the sentence is false.

False   **1.** Scientists know how many stars there are in the universe.

True   **2.** Spiral galaxies are the most common kind of galaxy.

False   **3.** The Milky Way is an elliptical galaxy.

False   **4.** Irregular galaxies have a definite shape.

True   **5.** The sun is in the Milky Way galaxy.

True   **6.** You can see the glow of the Milky Way on a clear night.

True   **7.** Spiral galaxies are shaped like a pinwheel.

False   **8.** Galaxies are moving towards each other.

True   **9.** Scientists think that a big bang created the universe.

False   **10.** Scientists know exactly how the universe began.

MATCHING

Match each term in Column A with its description in Column B. Write the correct letter in the space provided.

	Column A		Column B
b	**1.** Edwin Hubble	**a)**	our galaxy
d	**2.** irregular galaxies	**b)**	studied galaxies
c	**3.** spiral galaxies	**c)**	most common galaxies
e	**4.** elliptical galaxies	**d)**	least common galaxies
a	**5.** Milky Way	**e)**	shaped like a flattened ball

WORD SEARCH

The list on the left contains words that you have used in this Lesson. Find and circle each word where it appears in the box. The spellings may go in any direction: up, down, left, right, or diagonally.

STAR
GALAXY
ELLIPTICAL
SPIRAL
CONSTELLATION
BIG BANG
SUN
FUSION
SOLAR
MAGNITUDE

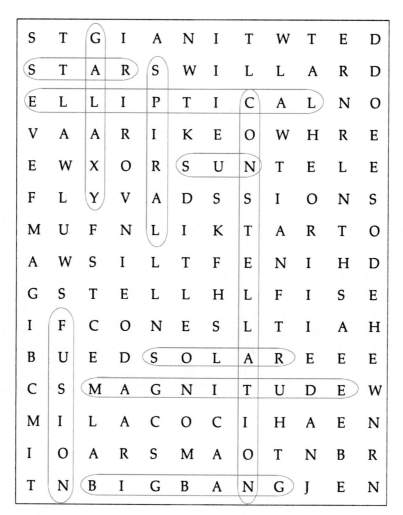

REACHING OUT

What force keeps all the stars in a galaxy together? Why? ___Gravity pulls all objects___

towards each other.

THE METRIC SYSTEM

METRIC-ENGLISH CONVERSIONS

	Metric to English	*English to Metric*
Length	1 kilometer = 0.621 mile (mi)	1 mi = 1.61 km
	1 meter = 3.28 feet (ft)	1 ft = 0.305 m
	1 centimeter = 0.394 inch (in)	1 in = 2.54 cm
Area	1 square meter = 10.763 square feet	$1\ ft^2 = 0.0929\ m^2$
	1 square centimeter = 0.155 square inch	$1\ in^2 = 6.452\ cm^2$
Volume	1 cubic meter = 35.315 cubic feet	$1\ ft^3 = 0.0283\ m^3$
	1 cubic centimeter = 0.0610 cubic inches	$1\ in^3 = 16.39\ cm^3$
	1 liter = .2642 gallon (gal)	1 gal = 3.79 L
	1 liter = 1.06 quart (qt)	1 qt = 0.94 L
Mass	1 kilogram = 2.205 pound (lb)	1 lb = 0.4536 kg
	1 gram = 0.0353 ounce (oz)	1 oz = 28.35 g
Temperature	Celsius = 5/9 (°F −32)	Fahrenheit = 9/5°C + 32
	0°C = 32°F (Freezing point of water)	72°F = 22°C (Room temperature)
	100°C = 212°F	98.6°F = 37°C
	(Boiling point of water)	(Human body temperature)

METRIC UNITS

The basic unit is printed in capital letters.

Length	*Symbol*
Kilometer	km
METER	m
centimeter	cm
millimeter	mm

Area	*Symbol*
square kilometer	km^2
SQUARE METER	m^2
square millimeter	mm^2

Volume	*Symbol*
CUBIC METER	m^3
cubic millimeter	mm^3
liter	L
milliliter	mL

Mass	*Symbol*
KILOGRAM	kg
gram	g

Temperature	*Symbol*
degree Celsius	°C

SOME COMMON METRIC PREFIXES

Prefix		*Meaning*
micro-	=	0.000001, or 1/1,000,000
milli-	=	0.001, or 1/1000
centi-	=	0.01, or 1/100
deci-	=	0.1, or 1/10
deka-	=	10
hecto-	=	100
kilo-	=	1000
mega-	=	1,000,000

SOME METRIC RELATIONSHIPS

Unit	*Relationship*
kilometer	1 km = 1000 m
meter	1 m = 100 cm
centimeter	1 cm = 10 mm
millimeter	1 mm = 0.1 cm
liter	1 L = 1000 mL
milliliter	1 mL = 0.001 L
tonne	1 t = 1000 kg
kilogram	1 kg = 1000 g
gram	1 g = 1000 mg
centigram	1 cg = 10 mg
milligram	1 mg = 0.001 g

CLOTHING PROTECTION • A lab coat protects clothing from stains. • Always confine loose clothing.

 EYE SAFETY • Always wear safety goggles. • If anything gets in your eyes, flush them with plenty of water. • Be sure you know how to use the emergency wash system in the laboratory.

 FIRE SAFETY • Never get closer to an open flame than is necessary. • Never reach across an open flame. • Confine loose clothing. • Tie back loose hair. • Know the location of the fire-extinguisher and fire blanket. • Turn off gas valves when not in use. • Use proper procedures when lighting any burner.

 POISON • Never touch, taste, or smell any unknown substance. Wait for your teacher's instruction.

 CAUSTIC SUBSTANCES • Some chemicals can irritate and burn the skin. If a chemical spills on your skin, flush it with plenty of water. Notify your teacher without delay.

 HEATING SAFETY • Handle hot objects with tongs or insulated gloves. • Put hot objects on a special lab surface or on a heat-resistant pad; never directly on a desk or table top.

 SHARP OBJECTS • Handle sharp objects carefully. • Never point a sharp object at yourself-or anyone else. • Cut in the direction away from your body.

 TOXIC VAPORS • Some vapors (gases) can injure the skin, eyes, and lungs. Never inhale vapors directly. • Use your hand to "wave" a small amount of vapor towards your nose.

 GLASSWARE SAFETY • Never use broken or chipped glassware. • Never pick up broken glass with your bare hands.

 CLEAN UP • Wash your hands thoroughly after any laboratory activity.

 ELECTRICAL SAFETY • Never use an electrical appliance near water or on a wet surface. • Do not use wires if the wire covering seems worn. • Never handle electrical equipment with wet hands.

 DISPOSAL • Discard all materials properly according to your teacher's directions.

CONSTELLATIONS

Name	Abbreviation	Meaning	Name	Abbreviation	Meaning
Andromeda	And	Chained Maiden	Indus	Ind	Indian
Antlia	Ant	Air Pump	Lacerta	Lac	Lizard
Apus	Aps	Bird of Paradise	Leo	Leo	Lion
Aquarius	Aqr	Water Bearer	Leo Minor	LMi	Little Lion
Aquila	Aql	Eagle	Lepus	Lep	Hare
Ara	Ara	Altar	Libra	Lib	Balance
Aries	Ari	Ram	Lupus	Lup	Wolf
Auriga	Aur	Charioteer	Lynx	Lyn	Lynx
Bootes	Boo	Herdsmen	Lyra	Lyr	Lyre
Caelum	Cae	Chisel	Mensa	Men	Table Mountain
Camelopardalis	Cam	Giraffe	Microscopium	Mic	Microscope
Cancer	Cnc	Crab	Monoceros	Mon	Unicorn
Canes Venatici	CVn	Hunting Dogs	Musca	Mus	Fly
Canis Major	CMa	Great Dog	Norma	Nor	Square (rule)
Canis Minor	CMi	Little Dog	Octans	Oct	Octant
Capricornus	Cap	Sea-goat	Ophiuchus	Oph	Serpent Bearer
Carina	Car	Keel	Orion	Orti	Hunter
Cassiopeia	Cas	Queen	Pavo	Pav	Peacock
Centaurus	Cen	Centaur	Pegasus	Peg	Flying Horse
Cepheus	Cep	King	Perseus	Per	Hero
Cetus	Cet	Whale	Phoenix	Phe	Phoenix
Chamaeleon	Cha	Chameleon	Pictor	Pic	Painter
Circinus	Cir	Compasses (art)	Pisces	Psc	Fishes
Columba	Col	Dove	Pisces Austrinus	PsA	Southern Fish
Coma Berenices	Com	Berenice's Hair	Puppis	Pup	Stern (deck)
Corona Australis	CrA	Southern Crown	Pyxis	Pyx	Compass (sea)
Corona Borealis	CrB	Northern Crown	Reticulum	Ret	Net
Corvus	Crv	Crow	Sagitta	Sge	Arrow
Crater	Crt	Cup	Sagittarius	Sgr	Archer
Crux	Cru	Cross (southern)	Scorpius	Sco	Scorpion
Cygnus	Cyg	Swan	Sculptor	Scl	Sculptor
Delphinus	Del	Dolphin	Scutum	Sct	Shield
Dorado	Dor	Goldfish	Serpens	Ser	Serpent
Draco	Dra	Dragon	Sextans	Sex	Sextant
Equuleus	Equ	Little Horse	Taurus	Tau	Bull
Eridanus	Eri	River	Telescopium	Tel	Telescope
Fornax	For	Furnace	Triangulum	Tri	Triangle
Gemini	Gem	Twins	Trigulum Australe	TrA	Southern Triangle
Grus	Gru	Crane (bird)			
Hercules	Her	Hercules	Tucana	Tuc	Toucan
Horologium	Hor	Clock	Ursa Major	UMa	Great Bear
Hydra	Hya	Water Snake (female)	Ursa Minor	UMi	Little Bear
			Vela	Vel	Sail
Hydrus	Hyi	Water Snake (male)	Virgo	Vir	Maiden
			Volans	Vol	Flying Fish
			Vulpecula	Vul	Fox

THE PLANETS					
Planet	Number of Moons	Distance From Sun	Diameter	Period of Rotation	Period of Revolution
Mercury	0	57,900,000 km	4,880 km	59 days	88 days
Venus	0	108,200,000 km	12,100 km	243 days	225 days
Earth	1	149,600,000 km	12,756 km	24 hours	365 days
Mars	2	227,900,000 km	6,794 km	25 hours	687 days
Jupiter	16	778,300,000 km	143,200 km	10 hours	12 years
Saturn	18	1,427,000,000 km	120,000 km	11 hours	309 years
Uranus	15	2,870,000,000 km	51,800 km	17 hours	84 years
Neptune	8	4,497,000,000 km	49,528 km	18 hours	165 years
Pluto	1	5,900,000,000 km	3,400 km	6 days 9 hours	248 years

MASSES OF THE SUN, MOON AND THE PLANETS	
Sun	2,000,000,000,000,000,000,000,000,000,000 kg
Mercury	330,000,000,000,000,000,000,000 kg
Venus	4,900,000,000,000,000,000,000,000 kg
Earth	6,000,000,000,000,000,000,000,000 kg
Moon	73,000,000,000,000,000,000,000 kg
Mars	640,000,000,000,000,000,000,000 kg
Jupiter	1,900,000,000,000,000,000,000,000,000 kg
Saturn	570,000,000,000,000,000,000,000,000 kg
Uranus	87,000,000,000,000,000,000,000,000 kg
Neptune	103,000,000,000,000,000,000,000,000 kg
Pluto	15,000,000,000,000,000,000,000 kg

		MAJOR MOONS			
Moon	**Planet**	**Distance From Planet**	**Diameter**	**Period of Rotation**	**Period of Revolution**
Moon	Earth	384,000 km	3,476 km	27 days	27 days
Phobos	Mars	9,000 km	11 km	8 hours	8 hours
Deimos	Mars	23,000 km	6 km	30 hours	30 hours
Io	Jupiter	422,000 km	3,640 km	42 hours	42 hours
Europa	Jupiter	671,000 km	3,000 km	85 hours	85 hours
Ganymede	Jupiter	1,070,000 km	5,280 km	7 days	7 days
Calisto	Jupiter	1,880,000 km	5,000 km	17 days	17 days
Tetheys	Saturn	2934,000 km	1,060 km	45 hours	45 hours
Dione	Saturn	377,000 km	1,120 km	66 hours	66 hours
Rhea	Saturn	527,000 km	1,512 km	108 hours	108 hours
Titan	Saturn	1,222,000 km	5,120 km	16 days	16 days
Iapetus	Saturn	3,561,000 km	1,460 km	79 days	79 days
Ariel	Uranus	192,000 km	1,160 km	60 hours	60 hours
Umbriel	Uranus	267,000 km	1,190 km	99 hours	99 hours
Titania	Uranus	439,000 km	1,610 km	9 days	9 days
Oberon	Uranus	587,000 km	1,750 km	13 days	13 days
Miranda	Uranus	130,000 km	320 km	34 hours	34 hours
Triton	Neptune	654,000 km	3,400 km	6 days	6 days
Nereid	Neptune	5,570,000 km	940 km	360 days	360 days
Charon	Pluto	17,500 km	750 km	6 days	6 days

PHYSICAL CONSTANTS
Astronomical Unit (AU) = 150,000,000 km
Lightyear = 9,500,000,000,000 km
Speed of Light = 300,000,000 m/s

SELECTED SPACE PROBES

Spacecraft	Country of Origin	Launch Date	Accomplishments (Highlights)
Luna 2	USSR	9/12/54	First spacecraft to reach Moon
Luna 3	USSR	10/4/57	First circumnavigation of Moon, first pictures of far side
Marina 2	USA	6/27/62	First interplanetary mission—Venus flyby
Ranger 7	USA	7/18/64	Impact with Moon, transmitted first close-up pictures
Marina 4	USA	11/28/64	First close-up pictures of Mars, measurement of atmospheric surface pressure
Luna 9	USSR	1/31/66	First successful lunar soft landing
Luna 10	USSR	3/31/66	First spacecraft in lunar orbit
Surveyor 1	USA	5/30/66	First U.S. soft landing on Moon
Lunar Orbiter 1	USA	8/10/66	First lunar orbiting survey vehicle
Venera 4	USSR	6/12/67	First data back from inside atmosphere of Venus
Marina 6	USA	2/24/69	Mars flyby, first high-resolution imaging of Mars
Venera 7	USSR	8/17/70	First data back from surface of Venus
Luna 16	USSR	9/12/70	Soft landing on Moon with return of samples to Earth
Mariner 9	USA	5/30/71	Mars orbiter, first global mapping of planet
Pioneer 10	USA	3/2/72	First Jupiter flyby
Venera 8	USSR	3/26/72	First chemical analysis of Venus' surface
Pioneer 11	USA	4/5/73	Second Jupiter flyby and first Saturn flyby
Mariner 10	USA	11/3/73	First flyby of Mercury, obtained Venus data en route
Venera 9	USSR	6/8/75	Data from surface of Venus and from orbiter
Viking 1	USA	8/20/75	First soft landing on Mars, also Mars orbiter, *in situ* analyses of surface and atmosphere
Viking 2	USA	9/9/75	Second soft landing on Mars, also Mars orbiter, *in situ* analyses of surface and atmosphere
Voyager 1	USA	8/5/77	Flybys of Saturn, Titan, many experiments
Voyager 2	USA	8/20/77	Flybys of Jupiter, Saturn, Uranus, Neptune, many experiments
Pioneer Venus Orbiter	USA	5/20/78	First radar mapping of Venus from orbit
Pioneer Venus Probe Carrier	USA	8/8/78	Atmospheric composition, radiation balance, cloud particle characteristics from four entry probes
Venera 11	USSR	9/9/78	Atmospheric and cloud composition of Venus, surface studies
Venera 13	USSR	10/30/81	Venus atmosphere and surface studies, detection of lightning discharges
Venera 15	USSR	6/2/83	Orbiting radar mapper of Venus surface topography
VEGA 1	USSR	12/15/84	Venus flyby, descent probe landing, balloon deployment plus passage through Halley coma, many experiments
VEGA 2	USSR	12/21/84	Venus flyby, descent probe landing, balloon deployment plus passage through Halley coma, many experiments
Sakigake	Japan	1/8/85	Solar wind interaction with Comet Halley
Giotto	ESA*	7/2/85	Closest approach to Halley nucleus, many experiments
Suisei	Japan	8/18/85	UV imaging of Halley hydrogen corona, comet plasma measurements
Magellan	USA	5/4/89	Radar mapping of Venus surface topography
Galileo	USA	10/18/89	Jupiter orbiter with atmospheric probe

*ESA = European Space Administration = a consortium of European countries

SPACE SHUTTLE MISSIONS

Mission	Takeoff	Landing	Crew
STS-1 Columbia	4/12/81	4/14/81	Robert Crippen, John Young
STS-2 Columbia	11/12/81	11/14/81	Joe Engle, Richard Truly
STS-3 Columbia	3/22/82	3/30/82	Jack Lousma, Gordon Fullerton
STS-4 Columbia	6/27/82	7/4/82	Tomas Mattingly, Henry Hartsfield
STS-5 Columbia	11/11/81	11/16/82	Vance Brand, Robert Overmyer, William Lenoir, Joseph Allen
STS-6 Challenger	4/4/83	4/9/83	Paul Weitz, Karol Bobko, Story Musgrave, Donald Peterson
STS-7 Challenger	6/18/83	6/24/83	Robert Crippen, Norman Thagard, John Fabian, Frederick Hauk, Sally Ride (first U.S. woman in space)
STS-8 Challenger	8/30/83	9/5/83	Richard Truly, Daniel Brandenstein, William Thorton, Guion Bluford (first U.S. African American in space), Dale Gardner
STS-9 Columbia	11/28/83	12/8/83	John Young, Brewster Shaw, Robert Parker, Owen Garriott, Byron Lichtenberg, Ulf Merbold
41-B Challenger	2/3/84	2/11/84	Vance Brand, Robert Gibson, Ronald McNair, Bruce McCandless, Robert Stewart
41-C Challenger	4/6/84	4/13/84	Robert Crippen, Francis Scobee, George Nelson, Terry Hart, James Van Hoften
41-D Discovery	8/30/84	9/5/84	Henry Hartsfield, Michael Coats, Steven Hawley, Judith Resnik, Richard Mullane, Charles Walker
41-G Challenger	10/5/84	10/13/84	Robert Crippen, Jon McBride, Kathryn Sullivan, Sally Ride, Marc Garneau (first Canadian in space), David Leestma, Paul Scully-Power
51-A Discovery	11/8/84	11/16/84	Frederick Hauck, David Walker, Anna Fisher, Joseph Allen, Dale Gardner
51-C Discovery	1/24/85	1/27/85	Thomas Mattingly, Loren Shriver, James Buchli, Elison Onizuka, Gary Payton
51-D Discovery	4/12/85	4/19/85	Karol Bobko, Donald Williams, Charles Walker, Jake Garn, Jeffrey Hoffman, David Griggs, Rhea Seddon
51-B Challenger	4/29/85	5/6/85	Robert Overmeyer, Frederick Gregory, Don Lind, Lodewijk van den Berg, Norman Thagard, William Thorton, Taylor Wang
51-G Discovery	6/17/85	6/24/85	John Creighton, Shannon Lucid, Steven Nagel, John Fabian, Daniel Bradenstein, Prince Sultan Salman al-Saud (first Arab in space)
51-F Challenger	7/29/85	8/6/85	Roy Bridges, Anthony England, Karl Henize, Story Musgrave, Gordon Fullerton, Loren Acton, John-David Bartoe
51-I Discovery	8/27/85	9/3/85	John Lounge, James van Hoften, William Fisher, Joe Engle, Richard Covey

Mission	Takeoff	Landing	Crew
51-J Atlantis	10/4/85	10/7/85	Karol Bobko, Ronald Grabe, David Hilmers, William Pailes, Robert Stewart
61-A Challenger	10/30/85	11/6/85	Henry Hatsfield, Steven Nagel, Bonnie Dunbar, James Buchli, Giuon Bluford, Ernst Messerschmid, Reinhard Furrer, Wubbo Ockles
61-B Atlantis	11/26/85	12/3/85	Brewster Shaw, Charles Walker, Rodolfo Neri (first Mexican in space), Jerry Ross, Sherwood Spring, Mary Cleave
61-C Columbia	1/12/86	1/18/86	Robert Gibson, Charles Bolden, George Nelson, Bill Nelson, Franklin Chiang-Diaz, Steven Hawley, Robert Cenker
51-L Challenger	1/28/86	*	Francis Scobee, Michael Smith, Ronald McNair, Judith Resnik, Ellison Onizuka, Gregory Jarvis, Christa McAuliffe
STS-26 Discovery	9/29/88	10/3/88	Frederick Hauck, Richard Covey, David Hilmers, George Nelson, John Lounge
STS-27 Atlantis	12/3/88	12/6/88	Robert Gibson, Guy Gardner, Richard Mullane, Jerry Ross, William Shepard
STS-29 Discovery	3/13/89	3/18/89	Michael Coats, John Blaha, James Buchli, Robert Springer, James Bagian
STS-30 Atlantis	5/4/89	5/8/89	David Walker, Ronald Grabe, Mary Cleave, Norman Thagard, Mark Lee
STS-28 Columbia	8/8/89	8/13/89	Brewster Shaw, Richard Richards, David Leestma, James Adamson, Mark Brown
STS-34 Atlantis	10/18/89	10/23/89	Donald Williams, Michael McCulley, Shannon Lucid, Ellen Baker, Franklin Chang-Diaz
SS-33 Discovery	11/22/89	11/27/89	Frederick Gregory, John Blaha, Manley Carter, Story Musgrave, Katherine Thorton
STS-32 Columbia	1/9/90	1/20/90	Daniel Brandenstein, Bonnie Dunbar, James Wetherbee, Marsha Ivins, David Low
STS-36 Atlantis	2/28/90	3/4/90	John Creighton, John Casper, David Hilmers, Richard Mullane, Pierre Thuot
STS-31 Discovery	4/24/90	4/29/90	Loren Shriver, Charles Bolden, Steven Hawley, Bruce McCandless, Kathryn Sullivan
STS-41 Discovery	10/6/90	10/10/90	Richard Richards, Robert Cabana, William Shepard, Bruce Melnick, Thomas Akers
STS-38 Atlantis	11/15/90	11/20/90	Richard Covey, Frank Culberson, Robert Springer, Carl Meade, Charles Gemar
STS-35 Columbia	12/02/90	12/10/90	Vance Brand, Guy Gardner, Jeffrey Hoffman, John Lounge, Robert Parker, Samuel Durrance, Ronald Parise
STS-37 Atlantis	4/5/91	4/11/91	Steven Nagel, Kenneth Cameron, Jerry Ross, Jay Apt, Linda Godwin

* Exploded after takeoff killing crew

GLOSSARY/INDEX

parallax [PAR-uh-laks]: shift of position an object seems to have when it is seen from two different points, 24

perigee [PER-uh-jee]: point at which the moon is closest to the earth, 94

perihelion [per-uh-HEEL-yun]: point in the earth's orbit where the earth and sun are the closest, 72

phases [FAYZ-uz]: changing shapes of the moon, 98

photosphere [FOH-tuh-sfeer]: inner layer of the sun's atmosphere, 132

Pole Star: Polaris, the star above the north pole, 168

prime meridian [muh-RID-ee-un]: imaginary line that runs north and south through Greenwich, England, 64

radio telescope: telescope that can receive radio waves from sources in space, 8

reaction: an opposing force that balances an action, 28

reflecting [rih-FLEKT-ing] telescope: telescope that uses a concave mirror to collect light and produce an enlarged image, 8

refracting [rih-FRAKT-ing] telescope: telescope that uses convex lenses to collect light and produce an enlarged image, 8

revolution [reh-vuh-LOO-shun]: the traveling of an object around another object, 52

rotation [roh-TAY-shun]: the spinning of an object on its axis, 52

satellite [SAT-uh-lite]: natural or artificial object orbiting a body in space, 5, 34, 126

solar eclipse [SOH-ler uh-CLIPS]: passing of the moon between the earth and the sun, 104

solstice [SAHL-stis]: day on which the North Pole points toward or away from the sun, 58

Southern Hemisphere: the part of the earth south of the equator, 56

space probe: a machine that is sent from Earth to study other objects in space, 36

Space Shuttle: reusable space vehicle, 40

spectroscope [SPEK-truh-skohp]: an instrument used to study the light coming from an object, 14

spectrum: bands of different colors of light, 14

spiral galaxy: galaxy with a thick center and flattened arms, 172

spring tide: tide that is higher and lower than normal tides, 121

telescope: an instrument that gathers and magnifies light; used to study the heavens, 8

terrestrial [tuh-RES-tree-uhl] planets: planets that are similar to Earth in their size and composition, 138

tide: daily change of the level of ocean water, 118

time zone: part of the Earth where it is the same time; the Earth has 24 time zones, 64

universe [YOO-nuh-vurs]: everything that exists, 2

waning [WAYN-ing]: after the full moon; as the visible part of the moon decreases, 99

waxing: after a new moon; as the visible part of the moon increases, 99